BAILIFFS
The Law and
Your Rights

John Kruse

No 1 in the Your Rights series

TheConsumer
ActionGroup
RECLAIM THE RIGHT

Series Editor: Marc Gander, CAG

PP

Contents

There are several ways into this book:
- You can see the inside front cover to find what is specific to you;
- You can use the topic index at page 165; or
- You can use the conventional chapter contents list below.

Disclaimer

© John Kruse and PP Publishing 2011   All rights reserved.
Book ISBN 9781858117119 EBook 9781858117157 Printed & typeset in the UK

Introduction

This book is designed for use by non-lawyers, whether they are indebted individuals facing bailiff action or those seeking to advise them. It will be assumed that the reader is either an individual or a sole trader or partner in a business facing bailiff action, and the text will describe matters from this perspective.

The book seeks to describe the law simply and clearly, looking at each stage of the bailiff procedure and describing the options available to each side. It will avoid reference to the mass of complex case law and statute law that applies to this archaic and often confusing field. Readers who want to know more about this will find further reading in the list at the end of this book.

The use of bailiffs to seize goods in order to enforce unpaid debt is probably the commonest way of bringing pressure to bear on individuals to get them to satisfy their liabilities. Nationally there are probably between four and five million bailiff's visits annually. It is thus a huge aspect of debt recovery, and has tended to grow in the last decade.

This expansion is partly because new forms have been invented (e.g. child support maintenance or congestion charge) and partly because the use of existing forms has been extended (e.g. encouragement to magistrates' courts to increase fine recovery by using bailiffs).

Although every effort will be made to keep the text simple and approachable, the area of bailiffs' law is inevitably technical. Alongside the conventional route of contents (see page 5) and chapters for those who want it, we have tried to make this easier for you in the coming pages and suggest that you follow this path through the book.

1. Identify the type of case you are involved in and the type of bailiff you are dealing with using Flowchart 1 on the inside front cover.

2. Follow that flowchart onto one of the four Flowcharts to identify where to read about what you can do at the stage you have reached. There's often more than you think.

Tips & Hints

Use the blue tabs to find these pages again if you need to.

3. Before you start, familiarise yourself with key words and phrases that cannot be avoided: definitions of the most important ones are on page 15 and a more detailed glossary is on pages 160-161. In the text, glossary words are blue.

Note

The reader will see on the inside front cover that there are currently eleven forms of distress actively in use, enforced by four different types of bailiff, with the law for each subtly different. Despite the differences between the various forms of seizure, there are various common principles running through every form of bailiff action which this book will examine in the following chapters.

There are many other debts that are also enforced by seizure of goods, including a variety of taxes and various fines and damages for which shipping may become liable. Because these are so rarely used, they will not be mentioned in this book.

A word of caution on magistrates' courts It is important for readers to avoid confusion over bailiffs instructed by magistrates' courts. When we refer in this book to magistrates' warrants, we will be talking about bailiffs enforcing fines.

Magistrates' courts also issue liability orders to councils in respect of unpaid council tax and business rates, and to the CSA for unpaid child support maintenance, but the procedure for enforcing these is covered by completely different legislation to the recovery of fines.

To begin with, the creditors, rather than the courts, instruct the bailiffs. Distraint for these liabilities is therefore not the same thing as distraint for a fine. Follow the flowchart from the type of debt that you are dealing with to the right type of procedure in the magistrates' court.

Conclusion

Many aspects of bailiff law create the potential for dispute. The law is complex and old-fashioned, having developed through hundreds of years' worth of small changes. There are plans to reform it - see Chapter 9 for more details.

Also this law may be applied in tense situations by individuals with no special legal qualifications. Even more significantly, perhaps, these individuals may be operating without direct supervision and under pressure to get results. There is ample opportunity for an uncertain and confusing law to be misunderstood or circumvented.

The approach of this book is simple. Individuals liable for debts are clearly under an obligation to pay them - but that should be at a rate that they can afford. If they refuse to pay, they will face enforcement, but that should be carried out fairly. Problems should not be exacerbated by incorrect procedures and improper charges.

Stage

BEFORE A VISIT Chapter 2 page 17

Are you correctly named on the documents? p17
Did you receive the claim form? p18
Have you already paid? p17

NO

Can you pay in full?

YES → p29

NO

BAILIFFS DUTIES Chapter 3 page 35

Codes of Practice they should follow p37
Your human rights p41
Is their action proportional to the size of the debt? p41
Have they acted against principles of Equality? p43

INITIAL VISITS Chapter 4 page 51

Where you warned? p52

NO

YES

When can they visit p53,54

Where can they visit? p55

LEVY/ SEIZURE Chapter 5 page 67

YES

Visit to seize goods p67

Can you resist? p69

NO

Was impounding done correctly? p69-74
Check notices, p74
Check inventory, p75

Agreement? p79

What can be seized p83-94

Goods seized legally?

STOPPING REMOVAL OR SALE Chapter 6 page 101

YES

Have you paid?

NO

Took too much? p105

Removal rights p104
Reentry can only be forced with permission of judge p105

3rd party goods, p86

CHARGES Chapter 7 page 111

Rules for fees and charges pages 111-115

Checking p116

County Court actions

Remedy

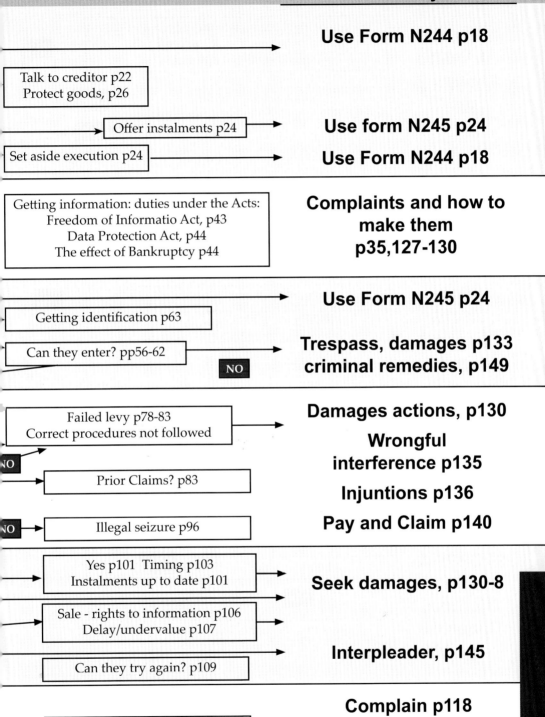

Use Form N244 p18

Talk to creditor p22
Protect goods, p26

Offer instalments p24

Use form N245 p24

Set aside execution p24

Use Form N244 p18

Getting information: duties under the Acts:
Freedom of Informatio Act, p43
Data Protection Act, p44
The effect of Bankruptcy p44

**Complaints and how to make them
p35,127-130**

Use Form N245 p24

Getting identification p63

Can they enter? pp56-62

NO

**Trespass, damages p133
criminal remedies, p149**

Failed levy p78-83
Correct procedures not followed

Damages actions, p130

NO

Prior Claims? p83

Wrongful interference p135

Injuntions p136

NO

Illegal seizure p96

Pay and Claim p140

Yes p101 Timing p103
Instalments up to date p101

Seek damages, p130-8

Sale - rights to information p106
Delay/undervalue p107

Can they try again? p109

Interpleader, p145

Complain p118

Challenging p117-120

Detailed assessment p118

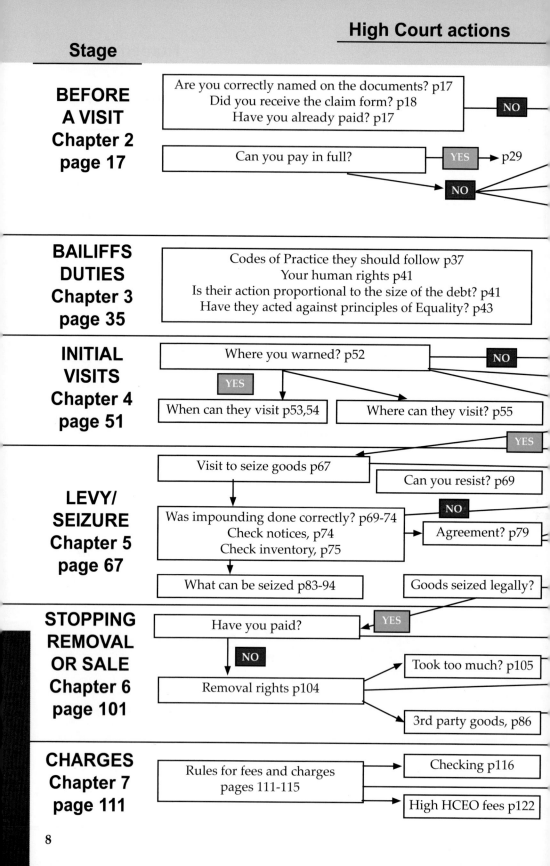

Stage

BEFORE A VISIT
Chapter 2
page 17

Are you correctly named on the documents? p17
Did you receive the claim form? p18
Have you already paid? p17

NO

Can you pay in full?

YES → p29

NO

BAILIFFS DUTIES
Chapter 3
page 35

Codes of Practice they should follow p37
Your human rights p41
Is their action proportional to the size of the debt? p41
Have they acted against principles of Equality? p43

INITIAL VISITS
Chapter 4
page 51

Where you warned? p52

NO

YES

When can they visit p53,54

Where can they visit? p55

LEVY/ SEIZURE
Chapter 5
page 67

YES

Visit to seize goods p67

Can you resist? p69

Was impounding done correctly? p69-74
Check notices, p74
Check inventory, p75

NO

Agreement? p79

What can be seized p83-94

Goods seized legally?

STOPPING REMOVAL OR SALE
Chapter 6
page 101

Have you paid?

YES

NO

Removal rights p104

Took too much? p105

3rd party goods, p86

CHARGES
Chapter 7
page 111

Rules for fees and charges
pages 111-115

Checking p116

High HCEO fees p122

Remedy

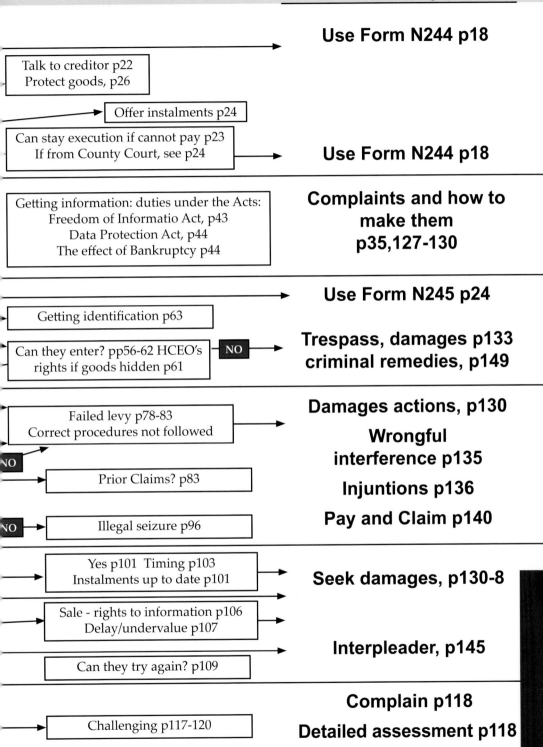

Use Form N244 p18

Talk to creditor p22
Protect goods, p26

Offer instalments p24

Can stay execution if cannot pay p23
If from County Court, see p24

Use Form N244 p18

Getting information: duties under the Acts:
Freedom of Informatio Act, p43
Data Protection Act, p44
The effect of Bankruptcy p44

Complaints and how to make them p35,127-130

Use Form N245 p24

Getting identification p63

Can they enter? pp56-62 HCEO's
rights if goods hidden p61

NO

Trespass, damages p133 criminal remedies, p149

Failed levy p78-83
Correct procedures not followed

NO

Prior Claims? p83

NO

Illegal seizure p96

Damages actions, p130

Wrongful interference p135

Injuntions p136

Pay and Claim p140

Yes p101 Timing p103
Instalments up to date p101

Seek damages, p130-8

Sale - rights to information p106
Delay/undervalue p107

Can they try again? p109

Interpleader, p145

Complain p118

Detailed assessment p118

Challenging p117-120

Private Bailiffs or Court's Enforcement Officer

Stage

BEFORE A VISIT
Chapter 2
page 17

Are you liable for local taxes or child support p19
Are you subject to a Magistrates' Court order? p20
Are you correctly named on the documents? p17
Have you already paid? p17

NO

YES

p29

Can you pay in full?

NO

BAILIFFS DUTIES
Chapter 3
page 35

Codes of Practice they should follow p37-39
Maladministration p40 Your human rights p41
Is their action proportional to the size of the debt? p41
Have they acted against principles of Equality? p43

INITIAL VISITS
Chapter 4
page 51

Did you receive a final warning? p52

NO

YES

When can they visit p53,54

Where can they visit? p55

LEVY/ SEIZURE
Chapter 5
page 67

Visit to seize goods p67

YES

Can you resist? p69

Was impounding done correctly? p69-74
Check notices, p74
Check inventory, p75

NO

Agreement? p79

What can be seized p83-94

Goods seized legally?

STOPPING REMOVAL OR SALE
Chapter 6
page 101

Have you paid?

YES

NO

Took too much? p105

Removal rights p104
Reentry can only be forced with
permission of judge p105

3rd party goods, p86

CHARGES
Chapter 7
page 111

Rules for fees and charges
pages 111-115
Magistrates' Court p112

Checking p116

Private Bailiffs or Court's Enforcement Officer

Remedy

Talk to the issuing Court

Protect goods, p26

Offer instalments p24   No instalments
Magistrates Court Orders p104

No assets?

Getting information: duties under the Acts:
Freedom of Informatio Act, p43
Data Protection Act, p44
The effect of Bankruptcy p47

**Complaints and how to
make them
p35,127-130**

Talk to the issuing Court

Identification rules p64

Can they enter? pp56-62

NO

**Trespass, damages p133
criminal remedies, p149**

Failed levy p78-83
Correct procedures not followed

NO

Prior Claims? p83

Offences re seized goods, p77

NO   Illegal seizure p96

Damages actions, p130

**Wrongful
interference p135**

Injuntions p136

Pay and Claim p140

Yes p101 Timing p103
Instalments up to date p101

Sale - rights to information p106, p109
Delay/undervalue p107
Return of goods after payment p104

Can they try again? p109

Seek damages, p130-8

Interpleader, p145

Challenging p117-120

**Complain p118
Child Support p144
Detailed assessment p118**

11

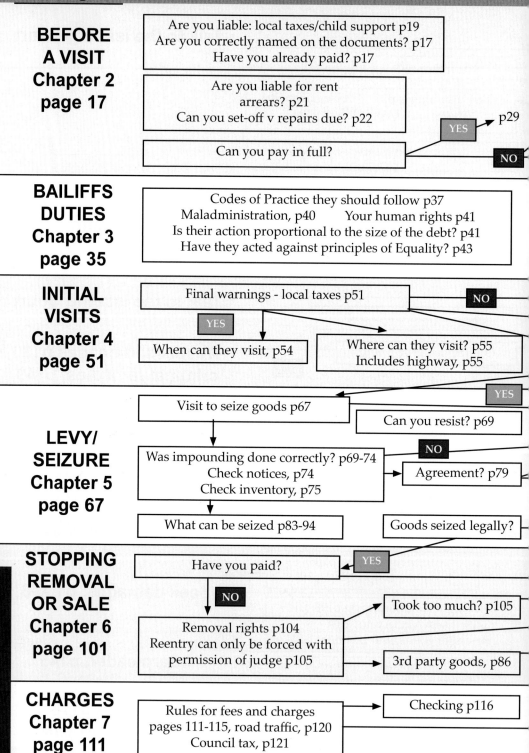

Stage

BEFORE A VISIT Chapter 2 page 17

Are you liable: local taxes/child support p19
Are you correctly named on the documents? p17
Have you already paid? p17

Are you liable for rent arrears? p21
Can you set-off v repairs due? p22

YES → p29

Can you pay in full?

NO

BAILIFFS DUTIES Chapter 3 page 35

Codes of Practice they should follow p37
Maladministration, p40   Your human rights p41
Is their action proportional to the size of the debt? p41
Have they acted against principles of Equality? p43

INITIAL VISITS Chapter 4 page 51

Final warnings - local taxes p51

NO

YES

When can they visit, p54

Where can they visit? p55
Includes highway, p55

LEVY/ SEIZURE Chapter 5 page 67

Visit to seize goods p67

YES

Can you resist? p69

Was impounding done correctly? p69-74
Check notices, p74
Check inventory, p75

NO

Agreement? p79

What can be seized p83-94

Goods seized legally?

STOPPING REMOVAL OR SALE Chapter 6 page 101

Have you paid?

YES

NO

Took too much? p105

Removal rights p104
Reentry can only be forced with permission of judge p105

3rd party goods, p86

CHARGES Chapter 7 page 111

Rules for fees and charges
pages 111-115, road traffic, p120
Council tax, p121

Checking p116

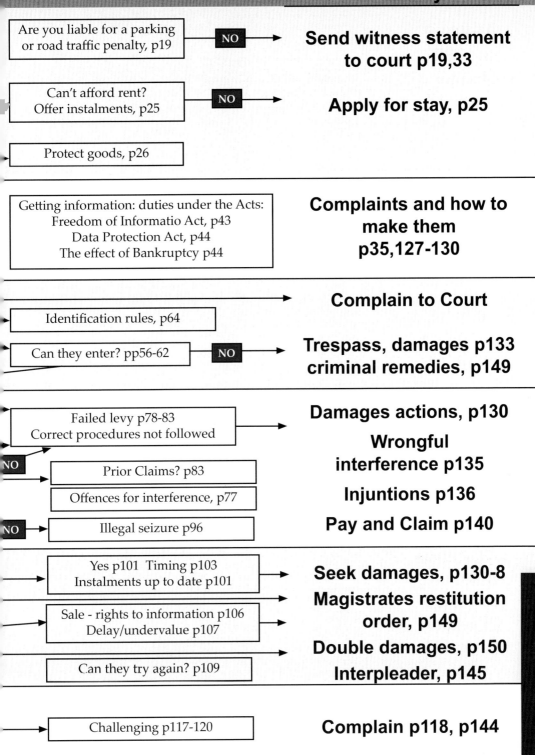

BEFORE A VISIT
Chapter 2
page 17

These officers have some specific powers, but otherwise see the County Court pages - 8-9

If you are not liable, assessment procedures p20

BAILIFFS DUTIES
Chapter 3
page 35

Codes of Practice they should follow p37
Maladministration, p40   Your human rights p41
Is their action proportional to the size of the debt? p41
Have they acted against principles of Equality? p43

INITIAL VISITS
Chapter 4
page 51

When can they visit, p54

For income taxes can force entry, p60

Where can they visit? p55
Includes highway, p55

LEVY/ SEIZURE
Chapter 5
page 67

What can be seized p83-94

Exempt goods,
VAT seizures, p91

STOPPING REMOVAL OR SALE
Chapter 6
page 101

As County Court

CHARGES
Chapter 7
page 111

As County Court

Chapter One: Key terms defined

A range of unfamiliar terms are used to describe the stages in bailiff actions. A quick reference glossary is included as Appendix One on page 159 and throughout the text where words in that glossary appear for the first time in a section these words are highlighted in blue. Please note though the following common words we will be using repeatedly:

Execution:

This refers to the seizure of goods by the county court bailiff or High Court enforcement officer (who is a private bailiff) to enforce a civil court judgment.

Readers should be aware that, even though a case might originally have been issued against them in the county court, it may end up in the High Court for enforcement. Any sum over £600 may be transferred for execution by a HCEO and many trade and utility debts are now recovered this was rather than using the county court bailiff service. Costs may be much higher.

The term execution also refers to the enforcement of local authorities' road traffic penalties by private, certificated bailiffs. The enforcement of road traffic debts is, technically, a form of execution as the orders for recovery are issued by a county court (the Traffic Enforcement Centre at the court in Northampton). The result is a strange hybrid remedy - county court execution being carried out by private bailiffs, albeit who hold a certificate issued by a county court judge (see chapter 8 later).

Confusingly one may also hear reference being made to 'executing distress'. This is because the word may also be used a verb, but the procedure being referred to will not be an 'execution' in the strict sense of the word.

Debtor/ creditor:

Although these terms can sound stark and harsh, they are convenient as they are shorter and simpler than 'person facing a bailiff's visit' and the like. The 'debtor' (properly 'judgment debtor') is the person held liable (rightly or wrongly) for the debt being enforced by the bailiff; the 'creditor' is the person or organisation owed money who has instructed the bailiff to call. As seen in Flowchart 1, the creditor may be a local authority or government department or may be a private landlord or a person who has obtained a court judgment (properly, a 'judgment creditor').

Distress or distraint:

This refers to any summary remedy involving seizure of goods outside the civil courts. Distress is also sometimes used as a term referring to the goods seized, the actual subject of the distress.

Enforcement agent:

It has become increasingly common to refer to bailiffs as enforcement agents. Partly this is to avoid the stigma attached to the older term, but it has two benefits: it reminds us that bailiffs act as 'agents' on behalf of a creditor (termed 'the principal', or client) who is liable for their acts and it also alerts us to the fact that, nowadays, bailiffs do more than just seize goods. Many firms will also be encountered performing arrest work as well for magistrates' courts and local authorities.

Levy:

This word will be frequently encountered. It is often interchangeable with the verbs 'distrain', 'seize' and 'execute (a warrant)'.

Possession:

This is now largely interchangeable with 'impounding'.

Seizure and impounding:

Are key phrases analysed later. In brief, however, they describe the process by which the bailiff asserts and retains his rights over the your goods. Readers should nonetheless note that the verbs 'to seize' and 'to levy' are largely interchangeable in everyday speech, although 'seize' has a technical meaning discussed in chapter 4.

Private bailiffs:

As you may have noticed, all bailiffs except the county court bailiff are 'private'. This means that they are offering their services to the creditor on a commercial basis, and will aim to raise their income from charging fees for the work they do, either to the creditor, or - most often - to you.

This 'profit motive' will inevitably influence their approach to their work, and make them more 'aggressive' than the court's bailiffs. Another aspect of this is that, as civil servants, the activities of county court bailiffs are more highly regulated and supervised than private firms.

As mentioned above, High Court enforcement officers are private bailiffs, though enforcing a civil court judgment, but because of their position as court officers and because the rules governing their activities are almost the same as those applicable to county court bailiffs, they may be regarded differently from those private firms levying distress.

Warrants:

The warrant is the instruction from the creditor to the bailiff to go out to collect the debt by seizing goods. In the county court, it is called a warrant of execution, and in the High Court, the same document will be encountered as a 'writ of *fieri facias*'. In other cases, it will be termed a distress warrant.

Chapter Two: Preventative Measures

Chapter Contents

Introduction

Most of the time dealing with a bailiff problem can be a matter of trying to put right what has already gone wrong. The bailiff has already called and seized goods, and is now in a position of strength. He will be able to demand payment, often a lump sum or high instalments over a short period. Without payment he can remove and sell the specific goods seized.

The only way of redressing the balance in a situation where the indebted person does not have the money (as is of course usually the case) may be to find some error in the proceedings. This is often not as difficult as it may sound, and will be the concern of the main part of this book which describes the successive stages of the process. Ideally, though, the preferable solution is to *avoid* the problem in the first place. This chapter looks at how bailiff action may be prevented.

It is worth reiterating that the basis of this book is that it is not an aid to avoiding legitimate debts. It is a guide to ensuring that the rules are applied fairly and that debts can be paid off at an affordable rate.

1. Challenging Liability

Enforcement may be prevented if the debt upon which the levy is based can be challenged. This will naturally invalidate any right to seize goods. Liability may be disputed for such fundamental reasons as that:

Q Quick Questions

1. Are you named?

2. Have you cleared the sum already?

  • the debt has been paid; or

  • you are not the person named in the warrant.

Such issues should be fairly easy to prove. There may also be more technical and legal defences available: these will tend to vary from debt to debt, as will the means of challenge that must be employed.

Judgments

If a court judgment is being enforced by execution, it may be possible to challenge it if you did not respond to the initial claim form. If you did try to defend the case, and were unsuccessful, this opportunity has plainly gone. However, if you didn't receive the claim form (which is not unheard of) or did not deal with it, the chance to fight the case is not lost totally.

It will be necessary to make application to the relevant court to have the judgment 'set aside' - in effect, cancelled. The court will do this where there is both a good reason for failing to respond the first time and you have a reasonable defence to the claim which should be heard by the court.

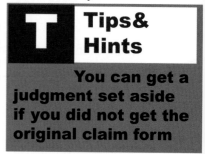

Tips& Hints

You can get a judgment set aside if you did not get the original claim form

If you are liable for the debt, and simply cannot afford to clear the debt at once, this is **not** a defence. You cannot set aside the judgment. Instead you should apply to stay (or freeze) the *execution* - see section 3 at page 23. On the other hand, if there is a valid basis upon which the claim may be contested - for instance a dispute as to liability or a counterclaim for damages, perhaps arising out of faulty goods or services, an opportunity should be given for these matters to be heard and you will need to apply for a set-aside.

Tips& Hints

Court forms are downloadable free from the Court Service Website - see page 165

Application to set judgment aside is on court form N244, for which a fee normally will be payable. (Court fees may sometimes be waived if you have limited income: visit your local court for more information.) The application to set aside will be heard by the court quite promptly. In the meantime the person should request that execution is stayed to prevent the bailiff taking any further steps.

If the judgment is set aside there will no longer be a debt that the court can enforce, and a further hearing will follow to consider the claim and defence.

If you apply for a setaside, it is a good idea to draft your intended defence and to give it to the court as part of your application.

A good move is to contact the creditor to ask if they will agree to your setaside application. They often will and then the setaside is almost automatically granted by the court and normally without a hearing. If your creditor does agree to a setaside, you should write to them confirming their agreement and copy the court. Even if they do not agree it is often worth applying as the courts may rule in your favour.

Bailiffs - The Law and Your Rights

Note that, if a judgment of the county court is being enforced in the High Court it will still be necessary to apply to county court to set it aside. If this application is made after enforcement of the judgment has been commenced, it may also be necessary for you to apply to the High Court to stay the execution (see section 3).

Liability orders

Local tax debts and arrears of child support maintenance are enforceable by distress once the council or CSA have obtained a Liability Order from the magistrates' court. This confirms the individual's liability for the unpaid debt. It is not like a judgment and is essentially a 'rubber stamping exercise' on the part of the court.

Q Quick Questions

Are you being chased for Child Support or council taxes?

Issues of liability should be taken up not with the court but with the creditor, who, if the challenge succeeds, should be invited to cancel or withdraw the order made.

Road traffic penalties

The procedure for getting a court order against you is as follows. A penalty may be imposed where an individual contravenes parking or moving traffic regulations (for instance, parking at a bus stop or stopping in a yellow box). The penalty is issued after you have been caught on camera or by a parking attendant either fixing notice on your car or giving it to you.

T Tips& Hints

Fixed Penalty Notices issued by public authorities are pursued like this, not private parking matters.

If you do not pay within 28 days, notice is served on you by the local authority stating that there are a further 28 days in which to pay or appeal and that the charge will increase thereafter. If you do not act then, a "charge certificate" is issued and the penalty increases by 100%. After a further 14 days the local authority may apply to the Traffic Enforcement Centre at Northampton county court for an order that it may recover the penalty as if it were payable under a county court judgment.

T Tips& Hints

See also PP Publishing's *Parking and Clamping Law*

You can challenge the original penalty charge notice after receiving it on a variety of set grounds, such as the fact that you were not driving the car or that the car was not your property at the time of the offence. You may later challenge the court order, on the grounds either that you did not receive the notice or that representations against it were ignored. This is done by sending a sworn 'witness statement' to the court.

Tips& Hints

Court forms are downloadable free from the Traffic Enforcement Website - see page 165

The effect of this is to revoke any county court order and cancel any charge certificate so the bailiffs cannot seize goods. Standard forms for this purpose may be obtained from the Traffic Enforcement Centre.

Magistrates' court orders

The magistrates' court may use distraint to enforce a range of orders.

Typically it will only be encountered being used to collect arrears on fines and other orders associated with criminal offences. Once the decision has been taken to use distress, it can be difficult to reverse (see 'suspending warrants' in section 3 later).

The only other way of challenging the remedy through the court would be to attack the original conviction upon which it is based. This may involve appeal either to the Crown Court or the High Court, and legal advice will normally be essential.

It is also possible for a person to appeal against the decision to enforce a fine, rather than against the imposition of the penalty itself. This is done by writing to the court's 'fines officer' stating why the decision should be varied and what the terms of any new order should be.

It will be essential to show good reasons why seizure of goods should not be used and to make a good repayment proposal at the same time.

Tips& Hints

In criminal cases, you can appeal the enforcement by offering reasons and proposing repayment

Other forms of distress

In every other case, no involvement with the court is required and the decision that a person is liable and that distress should be used is solely a matter for the creditor. In such cases any challenge to liability will have to be addressed to them directly.

Taxes

The basic rule is that arguments about an assessment cannot be raised as a defence to recovery proceedings. Instead, for both unpaid income tax or VAT, a process of appeal exists but it is likely that the liable person will have missed the first opportunity to exploit this, as matters will be well advanced.

Nonetheless, it is usually possible to appeal late, if good reasons can be shown for the delay. Recovery action may be suspended whilst liability is disputed. Details of the appeal process and the necessary forms may be obtained from your local tax office.

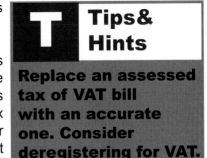

For both income taxes and VAT, tax due is assessed if a person fails to make an adequate return. When notified to the taxpayer this assessment is treated as the amount of tax due and recoverable, unless and until another figure is substituted. Clearly, in such cases it will be important for a person to replace an assessed bill with a correct one, which will almost always be lower. It is also worth noting that negotiations may be helped and enforcement withdrawn if a trader deregisters for VAT.

Rent

If the problem is rent, the only course of action may be to take up the matter directly with the landlord. Commercial landlords of business premises and local authority and housing association landlords of 'secure' tenants may use distress without any prior warning.

Negotiating with 'social housing landlords' over arrears should not normally prove too difficult because they all work under guidance from their professional bodies to the effect that, if distress is used at all, it should be used as a last resort in an effort to re-establish contact.

Commercial landlords (which may be private firms or public bodies) may be more of a problem to negotiate with as they will have few qualms about the use of the remedy, nor may they be particularly flexible about rates of repayment.

Landlords of assured and protected tenants may only use distress having obtained permission of the county court in advance (see section 3). This application to the county court will provide a forum at which issues of liability may be raised and any question as to liability is likely to lead to permission being refused.

For a landlord to be entitled to distrain, there must be arrears of rent, due on a current tenancy. Distraint cannot therefore be used if the tenancy has been terminated by forfeiture, by a court order or by a notice to quit. Distress cannot be used if new premises have been let to a tenant, if a new lease has been granted or if court action has been commenced for the arrears. If there are several tenancies in one tenant's name, each should be distrained for separately.

Preventative Measures

Service charges, water, fuel and insurance may be recovered by distress only if they are treated as rent by the lease or tenancy agreement - that is, it describes them as being 'reserved' or 'recoverable' as rent. If the agreement includes such items as part of the use of the land, the landlord can distrain for the whole balance due. The arrears must be certain, so if a service charge treated as rent is variable, the sum due must have been agreed by the tenant or otherwise confirmed (e.g. by tribunal).

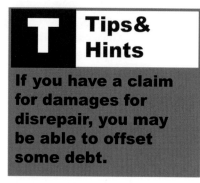

If you have a claim for damages for disrepair, you may be able to offset some debt.

Set-Off

If the landlord has not been maintaining your property properly, it may also be possible for the tenant to set off a claim for damages for disrepair against the arrears. The claim may be raised at the hearing for permission, or if there is none or you are too late for this, an injunction may granted to restrain a levy where the damages claim exceeds the rent due. Get two independent estimates of the work and use the lower of the two figures. Confronted with such a claim of disrepair, the bailiff can only take a provisional levy and refer it to the landlord.

2) Dialogue with your creditor

This may sound like a measure taken too late, but it may in some cases be more productive than trying to resolve matters with the bailiff directly. It is frequently the case for the bailiff to be instructed to collect the debt in a relatively short period of time. This will necessitate demands for the debt to be paid by large instalments. In some cases (fines and road traffic penalties are common examples) the instruction to the bailiff is to refuse anything but a lump sum payment of the total debt or very large instalments (see chapter 6 on terms of payment).

Where a person is on benefit or other low income, or has other personal or financial problems that may make such payment impossible, e.g. disability, recent bereavement or long term ill health, representations to the creditor based on these mitigating circumstances may be successful in agreeing a more affordable rate of payment. The creditor should then be expected to take payment directly and to withdraw the instruction from the bailiffs.

Tips& Hints

If you are on low income or have disability, ill health or bereavement issues, creditors - especially local authorities - may take this into account.

Alternatively, if you explain your personal or financial problems to the bailiff the warrant may be returned voluntarily. Many bailiffs, especially those acting for local authorities, operate under codes of practice which identify categories of person against whom distress should not be used. The bailiff will normally be expected to report back to the creditor for instructions, or return the warrant, as soon as it becomes apparent that the person visited falls into one of these categories of hardship (see chapter 3 on the National Standard and Equality Act).

If you decide to try and engage your creditor in dialogue, it is worth your while planning carefully what you think you want to say to him and what you might be able to offer him. You may feel that you have nothing to offer because you have so little money. This is not necessarily the case.

If you explain to your creditor that if he will help you make proper arrangements to repay the debt that this would save bailiff fees and other expenses, this would allow you to repay your debt to your creditor much more quickly.

You might even be able to point out to your creditor that enforcement action could possibly push you into bankruptcy which would then mean that none of your creditors would ever be fully paid.

Do not use this as a threat against the creditor - point out the logic of the situation.

3) Suspending warrants

It is possible to stop the bailiff by application to the relevant court.

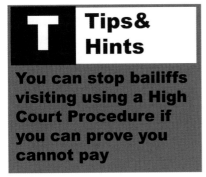

T Tips& Hints

You can stop bailiffs visiting using a High Court Procedure if you can prove you cannot pay

High Court stays of execution
Removal and sale of goods can be prevented by applying to the High Court for a 'stay of execution' of enforcement of the writ. This can be done soon after receiving the original claim form which demanded payment of the debt or after the HCEO has levied.

The court can stay execution if the conditions set out in court rules are met: "There are special circumstances which render it inexpedient to enforce the judgment" or if it appears that "the applicant is unable from any cause to pay money, then ... the court may by order stay the execution of the payment or order ... either absolutely or for such period and subject to such conditions as the court thinks fit".

Thus, the court can stay execution on terms of payment or impose a freeze for a set period to allow an application to set aside judgment to be made (see section 1 earlier).

Tips& Hints

Use court form N244 (see page 18) and samples of the right forms of statements on pages 32 and 33.

If an HCEO has already visited, application is on the Court's general notice of application (form N244) and should be accompanied by a statement of income and expenditure and assets, either sworn on an affidavit (see example at Sample 1) or presented in the form of a 'witness statement' (see Sample 2).

A fee is payable for the application, although you may be entitled to exemption. The court office can supply a leaflet and application form so that you can apply for fee remission.

Those on low incomes and certain benefits can have the fees waived. The affidavit of means needs to be sworn, which can be done at the Court or by a JP or commissioner of oaths. A small fee will also be payable for this.

Three copies of this application need to filed in the Court; it may be necessary at the same time to ask for the case to transferred to the Court nearest to you for hearing. The Court will set a hearing date; you must then send a copy of the application to the claimant by first class post, giving them at least four days' notice of the hearing.

In due course you will need to attend the Court for consideration of your application to take place. If you are successful in having enforcement stayed, you will need to draw up the court order yourself (see example at Sample 3). This needs to be taken or posted to the Court to be 'sealed' (stamped) and must then be served on the creditor.

If a stay is granted on a county court judgment being enforced in the High Court, a separate application will still be needed to the county court to vary the terms of that judgment (see next paragraph).

Suspending county court execution

Preventing execution is a relatively straightforward process for the defendant in the county court. It involves completion of court form N245, the application to suspend the warrant.

At the same time, an offer of repayment must be made, varying the existing instalment order if necessary, and the form allows a person to supply considerable detail of their income,

Tips& Hints

In the county court use court form N245 (forms page 166). You need to make an offer of payment.

expenditure and other liabilities in order to back up any offer. A court fee is payable by the defendant when the application is filed but may be remitted (see earlier).

The court will then arrange a hearing and notify the parties of the date (and the outcome).

Permission of court in distress for rent

As mentioned earlier a private landlord must obtain permission of the county court to use distress against a protected or statutory tenant under Rent Act 1977 or an assured or assured shorthold tenant under Housing Act 1988. At the hearing of this application, the court has powers to adjourn, stay or postpone proceedings. Permission to enforce should not be granted at all if there is a dispute as to the rent payable.

The court has absolute discretion in deciding whether or not to grant permission, therefore it is possible to suspend the order on conditions such as weekly payment of any arrears. Permission is also needed to levy against certain members of the armed forces. Otherwise, no prior court proceedings are required for a landlord to initiate distress for rent.

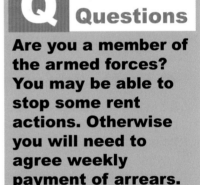

Q Quick Questions

Are you a member of the armed forces? You may be able to stop some rent actions. Otherwise you will need to agree weekly payment of arrears.

Postponement of issue by magistrates

On conviction in a criminal matter, a court may make a collection order regarding payment of the fine. This will specify the sum to be paid and the mode and rate of payment. A 'fines officer' will be allocated to oversee the fine's repayment; this person will be based at a court designated as the collections centre for a number of courts in a district. If the defendant defaults the fines officer can increase the fine by up to 50%.

If there is still no contact from the defendant, the fines officer can either refer the matter back to the court or issue a 'further steps notice'. A further steps notice can include the issue of a distress warrant or the issue to the bailiffs of a clamping order, which permits them to immobilise the defaulter's motor vehicle. If the matter is referred back to the court for a hearing, the magistrates can reduce the sum payable, vary the payment terms or order enforcement of the fine themselves, which could again include the issue of a distress warrant.

At the hearing stage, it is still possible for the court, if it thinks it 'expedient', to postpone the issue of a warrant until such time and on such conditions as it thinks just. Applications for postponement may be made as often as necessary.

However, there is no power to postpone or suspend a warrant once it has been issued. The courts have decided that once having issued (the warrant) the matter is out of the court's hands and the justices have discharged their duty and cannot intervene until the case is returned to them by the bailiffs. That said, in cases of hardship, it may still be worth contacting the court's fines officer to see if they will be prepared to assist.

Generally, both the fines officer and the magistrates should require evidence of the existence of distrainable goods before sending a warrant to the bailiffs. If the evidence reveals a 'reasonable likelihood' that there are distrainable assets, a warrant should be issued. The use of distraint as an option and the availability of seizable goods should always be considered by a court before imprisonment is threatened.

4) Protecting your goods

If the liability cannot be disputed or the warrant cannot be stopped, the distress may still be defeated by depriving the bailiff of anything that may be seized, though as noted above in criminal matters this may in the end lead to imprisonment.

There are a number of more or less sophisticated means by which this may be done. They are not necessarily convenient, easy or foolproof, but they have all been tried at different times. If you are determined to attempt something like this, you need to understand the practical and legal risks and problems.

Bills of sale

These are effectively mortgages on goods. In return for a minimum loan of £30 from a third party (who may of course be a friend or relative) a person gives his/her possessions as security. Various formalities and procedures must be exactly followed for bills to be effective against bailiffs. These include the form of the bill and its registration at the High Court. Noncompliance will mean that the goods are not protected and the bill will be void.

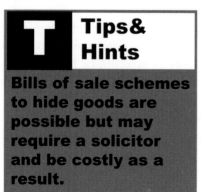

Tips & Hints

Bills of sale schemes to hide goods are possible but may require a solicitor and be costly as a result.

The effectiveness of a bill differs according to the debt being enforced by distress: execution and magistrates' court and local tax distraint are prevented. Income tax distraint may proceed as normal. Distress for rent by the landlord is not prevented, unless a Consumer Credit Act 'default notice' has been served by the lender.

It is clear that setting up a bill of sale is by no means easy and that most people will need to use the services of a solicitor - which will of course be costly. Even if a bill is properly made, the risk in such a course of action is still that the bailiff may choose to ignore the document and seize goods anyway, putting the onus of proving the bill on you. The matter would need to be resolved by a court and there is the risk that a judge might feel that even a perfectly valid bill of sale was made deliberately with the intention of putting assets beyond the reach of creditors and may refuse to uphold it.

Furniture leases

Another approach used from time to time is for a person to transfer his/her assets to a friend or relative and then rent the items back again, usually at a nominal rate. Although distress for rent would not be prevented by this technique if the transfer were to a spouse or business partner (as the landlord's basic right is to seize anything found at the rented property) in most other cases it should be effective. However, the courts may regard these arrangements as simply stratagems to avoid legal enforcement

T Tips& Hints

Transferring assets to another might work, but a court might deem them illegal so they are risky.

and refuse to uphold them in any claim brought by the owner for wrongful interference following seizure, just as with bills of sale above.

Hiding goods

There is nothing to stop you hiding goods around your home before the bailiff calls. It is not an offence and, as most bailiffs do not search with any great diligence or thoroughness, it may be successful. The only word of warning is that, just because on one visit the bailiffs are unsuccessful, does not mean that they have to give up and may never return. If they are suspicious that items are missing it would be permissible to simply try again later, when of course they might find that the hidden items have been retrieved from their hiding place.

T Tips& Hints

Hiding assets from bailiffs is possible. This includes motor vehicles but cameras may find them.

Motor vehicles may be 'hidden' by removing them from the immediate vicinity of the home. Readers should beware, all the same, as nowadays automatic number plate recognition (ANPR) potentially allows bailiffs to locate any car parked in any street.

Case Study

X moved his car when he knew Bailiffs were coming because the notice was for a 2 year old fine that was unknown to X. Moving it gave him time to apply for a stay.

If the registration number is known to the bailiffs (as in road traffic cases), the only safe option would be to park the vehicle out of sight of a public road on private land.

This strategy might be particularly useful if you know that there are valid reasons to set aside the judgment using procedures on pages 18 and 19. For example see the case study.

Removing goods

Along the same lines as the above, a person may pre-empt a bailiff's call by removing valuable items from the property. This is, in most cases, legal and will achieve the desired results.

Even though most bailiffs may levy anywhere that goods may be found in England and Wales, in most cases they will of course be unable to find out where else items might be located, only having the your home address. There are two situations in which you should proceed with more care.

Beware though. In distress for rent there is an offence called 'fraudulent removal'. This occurs when a tenant deliberately removes possessions in order to defeat a levy by the landlord, leaving insufficient goods for distress behind. The landlord can pursue and seize any goods which have been fraudulently or clandestinely removed within thirty days of their removal if they have not been sold in good faith.

Tips& Hints

Beware of removing too much - fraudulent removal is a criminal offence in rent cases.

There is a penalty for fraudulent removal of **double** the value of the goods removed. Alternatively a magistrates' court can impose a fine. It is fair to say, though, that this is an obscure and little used provision.

Secondly, readers should note that in execution the High Court enforcement officer or county court bailiff may pursue goods if they have been removed to third party premises to put them beyond their reach. The bailiff may also break into the third party's house in such cases. Demand for entry should be made first but force may then be used if entry is refused.

Both hiding goods and removing them from the premises are strategies that will work before a bailiff has called and levied. However, they involve the inconvenience of removing items to another location and the even greater inconvenience of not having their use for an unspecified period.

Whilst a bailiff collecting council tax may only retain the liability order for a few months, bailiffs recovering road traffic penalties have up to **one year** within which to execute the warrant. Hiding a car for this long may become a real endurance test. Lastly, remember that attempting to hide or remove goods **after** a levy is potentially an offence (see chapter 5) and is generally to be avoided.

Summary

Any effort to beat the bailiff must be exercised with considerable care and caution. Some of these strategies are really only feasible with legal assistance and careful legal advice should also be taken.

5) Payment in full

Tips & Hints

Payment of the debt and costs in full before the bailiff levies will terminate the process. The bailiff is obliged to accept the sums offered and cannot refuse to accept the correct amount.

Payment in full ends the procedure and makes any further action illegal.

If payment is made before seizure, any subsequent levy is illegal. In many cases this may not sound like realistic advice, as if such a lump sum were readily available, it would presumably already have been paid to the creditor. However, it may be argued that in some cases it is worth trying to raise money for such purposes as it will avoid the stress and cost of the bailiff's call.

For two kinds of debts, special rules apply to situations where the full sum due is paid:

magistrates' court
> Distraint cannot proceed if you pay or tender the sum on the warrant (plus costs) to the bailiff or if you present the bailiff with a receipt for the correct sum issued by the clerk of the relevant court; and,

local taxes
> If the sum due is paid or tendered before any distraint takes place, then goods cannot be levied. If only part has been paid the council can still issue distress for the balance. If only the court costs are unpaid, there is discretion whether or not to issue a warrant.

Payment can be made after a levy has started, but costs will have been incurred by the bailiff by then and you will be liable for these. This means that you will not be able to offer to pay the sum due and stop the enforcement whenever you like - see chapter 6 for more detail.

Conclusions

The important points to remember are:

- Prevention is always better than cure - try to negotiate
- Forward planning can safeguard your goods
- An overall solution to your problems may be better than a piecemeal one
- Always get advice before setting up a bill of sale.

Self-help solutions (for & against)

Remedy	Advantages	Disadvantages
Challenging debt	Likely to bar further enforcement	Liability difficult to challenge for many debts
Suspending warrant	Will permit affordable instalments in county court or High Court	Not possible for most bailiffs; Only possible in magistrates' court before warrant issued
Hiding items	Completely effective for small items	Not possible for cars etc! Unspecified duration, therefore inconvenient
Refusing entry	Completely effective except for tax and fines	A person needs will-power; May need to close windows or check visitors for an unspecified time
Removing items	Effective in most cases	Bailiffs can enter third party premises to search and HCEO can force entry to search; Fraudulent removal is an offence in distress for rent; Inconvenience
Disposing of items (bill of sale etc)	Transferring ownership will safeguard goods in most cases	Does not affect distress for rent; Time-consuming/ costly, especially bills of sale and leases; Bailiffs may refuse to accept; Courts may refuse to accept this remedy
Payment	Instalment payment will prevent removal; Lump sum will lift threat of bailiffs' visit completely	Terms/sums may be unaffordable; Walking possession is usually necessary first; Charges will accrue
Negotiate withdrawal with creditor	Will lift threat of distress; Better terms may be possible from creditor	Creditors often deny responsibility/control; Consent only in desperate cases

Sample 1
Affidavit of means in support of an application to stay execution

In the High Court of Justice
Queen's Bench Division
Claim no:

Between:

Creditor (Claimant)

v

You (Defendant)

Affidavit in support of stay of execution

I, (your name) of (your address), the above named defendant, make oath and says as follows:

1. On (date) the claimant entered judgment against me in the sum of £xxx, representing a debt of £xxx and costs of £xxx.

2. I am employed as (state occupation). My take home pay is £xxx monthly.

3. My wife is employed full time and has a take home pay of £xxx. She also receives Child Tax Credit of £xxx and Child benefit of £xxx. We have 2 children aged x and x. Our total monthly income is £xxx.

4. I have no assets of significant value. I rent my home from Anytown Borough Council. I own a car, registration Wxxx ABC, which is valued at about £350. I have no savings of any description.

5. My regular outgoings each month are as follows: (list)

6. I have other outstanding liabilities, in addition to the judgment debt in this claim, which are as follows (including the monthly payments I make towards them): (list)

7. In light of the above stated facts, I believe that my offer of payment of £xx monthly towards this judgment is a reasonable and affordable sum.

Sworn: this xx day of xx, 2011 *Signature*

Sample 2
Witness statement

The statement should be drawn up in the following form ,which is laid down in the court rules.

     (1) the party on whose behalf it is made,
     (2) the initials and surname of the witness,
     (3) the number of the statement in relation to
           that witness, and
     (4) the date the statement was made.

	Claim:
A.B. (and others)	Claimants
C.D. (and others)	Defendants

1) The statement should be expressed in the first person in the witness' own words and also begin by giving:
• the full name of the witness,
• your place of residence,
• your occupation, or if you have none, a description, and
• the fact that you are defendant in the proceedings.

2) A witness statement must indicate:
• which statements in it are made from the witness's own knowledge and which are matters of information or belief, and
• the source for any matters of information or belief.

3) A witness statement should be:
• produced on durable quality A4 paper with a 3.5cm margin,
• fully legible and should normally be typed on one side of the paper only,
• divided into numbered paragraphs,

4) It is usually best for each paragraph of a witness statement as far as possible to be confined to a distinct portion of the subject.

Statement of Truth

'I believe that the facts stated in this witness statement are true'.

Signature

Sample 3
Form of High Court order
staying execution

**In the High Court of Justice
Queen's Bench Division
Claim no:**

Between:

Claimant

v

Defendant

Before   Master XXX [Sitting in Private]

Claimant   (represented by ZZZ solicitors)

Defendant   (in person)

An application was made by the defendant on dd/mm/yyyy for execution of the judgment to be stayed on terms.

The Master read the written evidence filed and heard representations from the parties.

IT IS ORDERED that:

1. execution of the judgment is stayed;
2. that the defendant pay £xx monthly in discharge of the judgment debt; and,
3. that the costs of £xx be added to the judgment debt.

Dated: dd/mm/yyyy

Sworn: this xx day of xx, 2011   *Signature*

Chapter Three
Matters Common to All Bailiff Types

Introduction - complaints

If you feel that you have been poorly or wrongfully treated, you should complain.

It is always better to do this in writing, rather than by phone. There are several reasons for this:

▶ you will be able to set out what you want to say clearly and fully;

▶ you will be able keep a record of what you said; and - last but not least –

▶ someone more senior in an organisation is likely to deal with the matter.

There is seldom little to be gained by complaining to the bailiff on your doorstep about his behaviour! He may not understand the law adequately, he may be reluctant to admit he has made a mistake and - if nothing else - you will be running up your phone bill with little to show for it! If there is a witness a polite but firm complaint may be worthwhile for future purposes.

If your first letter is ignored, or you are dissatisfied with the response, write again and/ or go higher up in the organisation.

This chapter looks at some of the general procedures and principles applicable to creditors and their enforcement agents to enable you to complain and challenge. It helps you identify where to go for more information if you need it. Chapter 8 considers in detail the various remedies available to you – how you challenge.

Tips& Hints

A key theme of this book is if you feel that something has gone wrong, complain and be persistent

Sources of the law

One of the major problems with enforcement law (and one of the reasons for this book) is that it can be very hard to discover what the law actually says. This is the result of the fact that there are so many different forms of seizure of goods and is due to the fact that bailiff law has been developing over centuries and has not yet been modernised by Parliament (but see page X, Chapter 9).

This book aims to be a simple and comprehensive source of reference for readers without any particular legal knowledge. You don't have to know more – and it may be the case that if you feel you should, that's the time to get advice from an expert at a CAB or from a lawyer.

However, if you want to research the subject further a reading list is provided as Appendix 4 which will guide you to the many sources of the law controlling what bailiffs can and cannot do; websites are listed there too. These include:

Legislation:
Most forms of seizure of goods are now wholly, or at least partially, regulated by rules laid down by Parliament. These will be found in the Acts of Parliament dealing with the collection of particular debts. Often these are supported by detailed 'statutory instruments' - sets of rules and regulations which set out the precise procedure to be followed by bailiffs.

Ask the creditor or bailiffs what powers they act under: often, you will find this information on the documents you have received. You can then inspect the relevant legislation on the website of the Office of Public Information.

The rules for magistrates courts and for the county court and High Court are also available online - see the Court Service website for the Criminal Procedure Rules (Part 52 deals with fines distraint) and the Civil Procedure Rules (Part 75, for instance, deals with parking penalties). All this information is free.

Case law:
All legislation requires interpretation by the courts to explain how it should be applied in specific cases. The most important decisions are those made in the High Court, the Court of Appeal and the Supreme Court. This book mentions only a few recent and significant cases by name, but there are many thousands which determine the rights and duties of bailiffs and debtors.

A good starting point for research is the (free) website of the British and Irish Legal Information Institute (BAILII).

Guidance & codes of practice:
Many central and local government departments issue their own guidance as to how the relevant law should be understood or applied (see page 37, and in Chapters 4-7).

Contracts:
The contract or service level agreement between the creditor and the

enforcement agency may specify how the relevant law should be understood or applied (see below).

Codes of practice -
the National Standard & others

Codes of conduct which supplement the written law exist at both local and national levels and can be useful tools in negotiations with bailiff companies and creditors.

National codes of practice

Two nationally applicable codes of practice apply to bailiff firms. The first is the National Standard for Enforcement Agents, which was issued by the Lord Chancellor's Department in 2002.

Tips& Hints

Bailiffs should act according to published codes of practice

It lays down minimum standards for all agents collecting all types of debt; all the key 'stakeholders' in the sector committed themselves to supporting it - these include the Local Government Association, all the bailiff trade bodies and the Institute of Rating, Revenues & Valuations which is the professional association for local authority collection staff.

Although it is nearly a decade old, the National Standard continues to be applicable and firms, individual bailiffs and local and central government creditors should all respect it.

Tips& Hints

If you are, or are advising, a vulnerable individual, the Standards will be useful to you

An outline of the key elements is given in Appendix 2, page 162. Throughout the text, relevant provisions will be mentioned at the appropriate point. The Standard is especially helpful for the protection it gives to 'vulnerable' individuals. The law does not generally offer any special status to those who are mentally or physically ill, disabled or otherwise disadvantaged, so the provisions in the Standard can be extremely valuable.

If the Standard is not respected, this could form the basis of a complaint to the bailiff firm or council/ government department, with the possibility of taking the complaint further if it is not dealt with satisfactorily. A complaint against the bailiff's personal certificate might be another option in a serious case (see chapter 8).

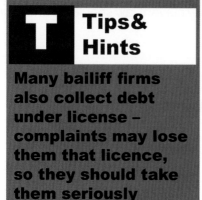

Tips& Hints

Many bailiff firms also collect debt under license – complaints may lose them that licence, so they should take them seriously

Secondly, many of the larger private bailiffs' companies will be licenced by the Office of Fair Trading (OFT) under the Consumer Credit Act 1974. This licence is not required for their bailiff work, but is necessary if they wish to undertake general debt collection, which many firms also do.

If a firm holds a consumer credit licence, it will have to comply with the debt collection guidelines laid down by the OFT. These were devised primarily to lay down best practice for debt collection agencies collecting credit and utility debts, but they can be applied to usefully to bailiff work as well, although readers will need to bear in mind that appropriate amendments will need to be made: bailiffs have legal powers which debt collectors do not.

A summary of the OFT code is included in Appendix 3, at page 164. If it is felt that a bailiff company holding a licence is not complying with the guidelines, an initial complaint should again be made to the firm, but the ultimate sanction would be to raise the matter with the OFT.

Local codes of practice

It is very common these days for local authorities and central government agencies to impose codes of practice on bailiffs as part of the contract agreed between them.

Tips& Hints

Why knowing a local code can be useful

Many codes are well-drafted and offer considerable protection in addition to that laid down in the law, both by exempting vulnerable groups and by expanding upon the present legislation or by clarifying or defining the law where it is either unclear or even absent. Typical terms in codes include the conduct of levies, the treatment of certain groups (such as those on means tested benefits), extra categories of protected goods and extra limits upon charges that may be made. Look at the Consumer Action Group section on the inside back cover for details of the forum which publishes these when they are obtained.

That said, there can be problems with codes:

► In many local authorities codes are regarded as internal only, part of the private contract between local authority and bailiff. As a result, they may not be published – the CAG has had considerable difficulty obtaining some even through Freedom of Information requests. If not published, they are of little use to indebted individuals as a means of controlling bailiffs' activities.

There may be scope for a Human Rights Act challenge here, as other public bodies who have interpreted their powers through unpublished guidance have been criticised by the European Court of Human Rights. Where a document deals with how a person's rights may be interfered with, the Court has decided that the document should be accessible to individuals.

▶ Furthermore in several cases known to the author codes have endorsed practice by bailiffs that were either illegal or of dubious legality. Whatever the contents of any contract or code between bailiff and creditor, it cannot authorise illegal acts and with the bailiff acting as agent for the creditor, both will be liable for any wrongful act (see chapter 8)

The value of codes of practice is the extra assistance and protection given to people, especially those in vulnerable circumstances. Also, once again, the moderating influence that the provider of the code may have upon debtor and bailiff relations. It is worth checking local authority websites to see which code has been adopted.

The problem with codes is that they can often be drawn up as public relations exercises, but are then often neglected. They are only as strong as individuals and advice agencies make them, so any perceived breach must be taken up.

Contracts

As well as codes of practice, the contracts between creditors and their enforcement agents may impose extra restrictions on the bailiff's conduct or may add extra protection for special groups.

Two nationally applicable contracts provide examples of such provisions. Both the Child Support Agency (CSA) and the HMCS (Court Service) contract for fines recovery identify vulnerable groups with whom extra care is needed. These include:

▶ Elderly people who have difficulty managing their affairs;

▶ The long term sick or disabled, especially those currently or recently hospitalised;

▶ Pregnant women; and,

▶ Those with mental disabilities or who have communication problems.

> **Q Quick Questions**
>
> **Are you in a vulnerable group? You may be protected by contract.**

In all such cases, the bailiff is required to obtain further instructions from the creditor before proceeding with a levy.

The Child Support Agency also makes stipulations about the following aspects of procedure:

► Categories of goods which should be treated as exempt from seizure. For example, the CSA list includes first aid equipment; prams, buggies and other items for the care of a child; items like wheelchairs used by disabled individuals; cleaning equipment (vacuums and washing machines); cooking utensils; essential business vehicles and equipment and educational equipment (which is defined as excluding personal computers);

Tips& Hints

The CSA cannot seize childcare equipment. Or other equipment that relates to caring

► Reasonable times for visiting (7am to 9pm and not on Sundays or holidays); and,

► The need for permission to be obtained from CSA before removal of goods for sale.

A Freedom of Information Act request (see page 43 below) for a copy of the relevant contract may well reveal other such provisions. Not to comply may be maladministration, which can be complained about as explained below.

Readers should note that contracts may sometimes also include clauses endorsing activities by bailiffs which are not lawful (additional fees is a good example which is discussed on pages 111 to 127 below). If any such terms are found, complain to the council department or your councillor.

Maladministration

The majority of the creditors who will be instructing bailiffs to pursue alleged debtors will be public bodies - central and local government departments. They are all required to comply with certain principles of 'public' or 'administrative' law, as are the bailiffs acting for them. These include the duty to act within their lawful powers at all times, to follow the law correctly and to give reasons for their decisions.

Failure to act properly, along with general poor administration and customer care, are all issues which may be the subject of complaint, initially to the public body in question, but ultimately to the ombudsman service which oversees the department.

Readers should obtain a copy of the complaints procedure operated by the public body in question. This will generally be publicised on its website.

If a complaint to a local council cannot be resolved satisfactorily, the matter may then be taken up with the Local Government Ombudsman. For central government departments, the Parliamentary Ombudsman or certain special adjudicators exist. Full details of the procedures are published on their websites (see Appendix 4).

Human rights is a special aspect of administrative law and is discussed separately in the next section.

Human rights & bailiffs

The Human Rights Act 1998 incorporated directly into English law the European Convention on Human Rights (ECHR). This did not change English law, as the UK has been subject to the ECHR for the last 50 years, but it did make it easier for citizens to assert their human rights against 'public authorities' in England and Wales.

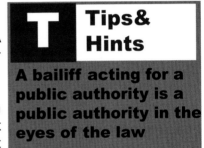

A public authority is any local or central government body (including the likes of CSA and the courts) as well as those acting on their behalf (such as bailiff companies).

A bailiff acting for a public authority is a public authority in the eyes of the law

It might be imagined by readers that the Human Rights Convention has a great deal to say about the protection of individuals from enforcement action by the state. In fact, this is not the case.

The relevant 'articles' (rights) in the Convention are articles 8 and First Protocol, article 1, which respectively protect the home and a person's possessions. In both instances, exceptions are made in favour of the state, permitting it to enforce taxes, fines and judgments provided that this is "in the public interest" and that everything is done "in accordance with the law."

It follows that, as long as bailiffs act lawfully, there is little in the ECHR which will directly prevent them. In fact, the European Court of Human Rights has gone as far as to say that the upset and loss caused by enforcement action is an inevitable part of that process. Many judgments of the Court in Strasbourg have also confirmed that the rights of creditors are as important as the rights of debtors.

All the same, we should not jettison the ECHR entirely. Whilst the rights themselves may not offer much protection from enforcement action, one of the principles which the Court uses when interpreting and applying the rights in the Convention may still be extremely useful. This is the concept of '**proportionality**'.

Proportionality is the idea that, in deciding whether to interfere with a person's rights, the public authority must balance the wider public need against the impact on the individual. Whilst it is accepted that taxes and court orders should be paid, the means of achieving that end chosen by the public authority should be the one that has the least damaging consequences for the person in debt.

For example, local authorities collecting council tax and magistrates' courts enforcing fines have a range of enforcement methods available to them. They should apply proportionality when choosing whether to send in the bailiffs or whether to make deductions from benefits to recover the arrears due.

If the authority chooses to instruct bailiffs, proportionality will apply at several points throughout the levy process: it may be disproportionate to continue to levy against a person who is obviously very poor and vulnerable; it will be disproportionate to seize a very large number of goods to cover a very small debt (see chapter 8 later).

C **Case Study**

By way of example of these principles being applied, we may refer to the case of *Anthony Brookes v Secretary of State for Work & Pensions and the Child Maintenance & Enforcement Commission* [2010].

Mr Brookes challenged the decision of the CSA to issue distraint for arrears of child support maintenance when they had already secured the debt against his house by means of a 'charging order.'

The Court of Appeal agreed that the CSA must take into account the welfare of the children when deciding how to enforce arrears, but it felt that sending in the bailiffs was less disproportionate than starting proceedings to try to sell the house.

The public interest in enforcing outstanding arrears and the fact that Mr Brookes had paid nothing at all off his

debt had to be balanced against the interests of the children in the household.

Moreover, the simple fact that bailiffs might call at the house did not automatically mean that there would be any loss to the children.

If you feel that the human rights aspect of your case has not been adequately addressed, the starting point will be a complaint to the public body in question. This may then be pursued up to the relevant ombudsman service if it cannot be resolved initially. Judicial review in the High Court may also be an option, but this should only be selected with legal advice and with legal aid support.

Equality Act

The Equality Act 2010 imposes on public authorities, in particular, a duty to avoid discrimination in the course of its activities. This duty applies not only to a central or local government department but also to those performing 'public functions' on behalf of public authorities - this seems very clearly to include private bailiff companies providing their services for the collection of public debt.

Not only should discrimination be avoided; organisations should also take steps actively to improve their services, policies and facilities to ensure that they operate in the least discriminatory manner possible.

Q Quick Questions

Has the body instructing the bailiff acted positively to avoid discrimination?

Discrimination under the Act is defined as being any less favourable treatment which a person receives on the basis of age, disability, gender, sexual orientation, pregnancy or maternity, race or religion. It will be seen that some aspects of the National Standard already make recommendations on these issues (see page 37 above).

Freedom of information

Individuals now have a number of rights to obtain information held by organisations.

These are useful to those involved in disputes about enforcement action as they can help establish:

▶ The rules of procedure applicable to the bailiff; and,

► The evidence available as to the bailiff's actions in a particular case.

A person is entitled to obtain disclosure of the information under two different Acts of Parliament:

Freedom of Information Act
This Act enables an individual to request from a public body (such as a local authority or central government department) all the documents it holds on a specified topic.

For example, in cases of bailiffs' disputes, it may be helpful to address to the council a request for copies of all the documents it holds which regulate its relationship with its enforcement agents - that is, its contract or service level agreement and any code of practice which may apply.

Use an FoI request to find out what codes and contracts apply between a public body and the bailiff instructed by them

This will reveal what limits (if any) have been imposed on the bailiffs' activities over and above the legislation applicable. A Freedom of Information request must be made in writing, specifying the applicant's name and address and the information required. This may be done by post or by e-mail. Some public bodies have ready prepared enquiry forms for you to fill in on their websites.

Data Protection Act
A person is entitled to ask any organisation to disclose to it the information it holds about him/her. This is done by means of a so-called 'subject access request'. A sample form is included at page 50 as Sample 4. This permits to disclosure of not only paper files but also computer records.

Obtaining the bailiffs' record of their activities on a case may be extremely valuable when examining fees (see chapter 7 later).

Insolvency

The insolvency of a debtor has a major impact on the ability of the bailiff to proceed and will generally be a complete bar on any further progress with a levy. Of course, bankruptcy or the like is a major step to take and should not be considered solely as a remedy to the threat of bailiffs, but it can be a solution to serious multiple debts and will provide an overall answer that deals with every competing demand upon your resources.

Although it is a desperate measure, in the context of un-payable and insurmountable debts, insolvency may be a complete resolution.

The various forms of insolvency and their impact on debt enforcement are described in the following sections.

Individual Voluntary Arrangements

The individual voluntary arrangement (IVA) enables individuals who are in debt or facing insolvency to agree with their creditors proposals for the reorganisation of their finances in order to avoid being made bankrupt. Creditors are offered a scheme of repayment that should leave them better off than if the person went bankrupt, and the debtor avoids all the stigma and restrictions of actually being an undischarged bankrupt.

Tips& Hints

IVAs initially protect debtors from bailiff action for 14 days

IVAs can only be set up with the help of an Insolvency Practitioner (IP) and this can often make them too expensive for many people. However they have the advantage that enforcement is affected at two stages.

The initial stage of the procedure is for the person to formulate repayment proposals with the IP who acts as 'nominee' and draws up a detailed scheme for presentation to the creditors. To buy time for this work to be done, the IP can apply to the court for an 'Interim Order.' The Order lasts for 14 days initially and allows the nominee time to prepare a report for the court on the IVA proposal.

The effect of an Interim Order is to establish a moratorium during which no execution or other legal process may be commenced or continued and no distress may be levied, except with leave of court. This provides comprehensive protection for the debtor from all forms of enforcement action, including all sorts of bailiff recovery.

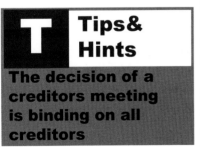

Tips& Hints

The decision of a creditors meeting is binding on all creditors

Before the expiry of the Interim Order the nominee must report to the court whether a creditors' meeting should be summoned to consider the IVA.

If the court is satisfied from the report that the debtor has a scheme likely to satisfy his/ her creditors the order is extended to permit the creditors to meet. The nominee sends details to all creditors and invites them to meet to vote upon the proposals.

If 75% by value accept the scheme it comes into effect and all unsecured creditors are bound by it. This means that they must accept the repayments and cannot enforce their debts whilst the IVA is in force and the debtor is complying. As a consequence, no further bailiff action at all will be possible.

Bankruptcy

Bankruptcy is precipitated by the presentation of a 'petition' either by the debtor or by a creditor. If the court is satisfied that a debt is due and that the debtor is unable to pay, a bankruptcy order will be made.

The making of a bankruptcy order has a number of effects on the bankrupt person's finances and property. It largely takes away the person's control of their affairs and places the administration in the hands of a trustee, whose main job is to seek to raise what money can be recovered from the bankrupt's estate - his/ her assets and income - so as to pay the creditors.

However, in return, debtors are given substantial protection from enforcement by their creditors, as will be described later.

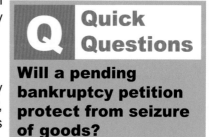

Quick Questions

Will a pending bankruptcy petition protect from seizure of goods?

Pending Petitions:
Whilst a petition is pending the bankruptcy court may, on application from the debtor, stay any execution or other legal process against the property or person of the debtor.
Equally the court where the case is taking place, for instance a magistrates' court dealing with a Liability Order application, may stay proceedings or allow them to continue on terms.

The courts have decided that the term "other legal process" does not include most bailiffs' visits. In short, court action and execution of judgments may be prevented whether in a civil court or criminal court, but the debtor will have to make an application to the court for this protection, and the court cannot inhibit distraint.

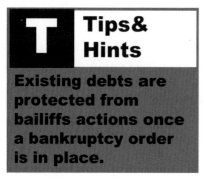

Tips& Hints

Existing debts are protected from bailiffs actions once a bankruptcy order is in place.

Effect of Order:
After a bankruptcy order is made no creditor whose debt is provable (i.e. included) in the bankruptcy may take any steps against the person or property of the bankrupt. Property includes goods, chattels and money. The effect of this is to completely bar enforcement of an existing debt. These restrictions on enforcement are, however, subject to special rules applying to distraint and execution - see later.

If new debts arise the situation is more complex. If there are no existing debts proved for in the bankruptcy then the creditor can proceed with recovery action as normal save that enforcement could be stayed on application to court by the bankrupt in the same manner as described for pending petitions. In most cases there may be little reason to bar enforcement as bankruptcy does not absolve a person of responsibility for ongoing or subsequent liabilities.

However if the creditor already has a debt included in the bankruptcy, permission of court is required to pursue any debt arising later. Presumably, the purpose of this is to prevent any harassment of bankrupts by aggrieved creditors.

Distress for rent:
Even after a bankruptcy order, there is a limited right of distress for a landlord.

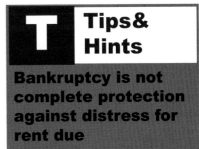

Generally, rent arrears are unenforceable after bankruptcy and will have to be proved for like every other debt of the tenant. However, the landlord may still distrain for any rent due for the six months immediately prior to the beginning of the bankruptcy, which is the date when the order was made.

The landlord may distrain even though the property is vested in the trustee, but if there are no goods, the only remedy is to claim for the rent in the bankruptcy. The protection against the landlord's distress offered by the bankruptcy interestingly extends after discharge.

Even then, the landlord cannot distrain upon any of the goods that were comprised in the bankrupt's estate.

Other distraint:
None of the restrictions affecting landlords or bailiffs levying court executions apply to other forms of distraint. Bailiffs may therefore proceed to levy against a bankrupt for local taxes, income taxes and VAT as normal.

It is understood that HMRC do not exercise their rights to levy unless, respectively, the debtor continues to trade and incurs further debts or if other creditors also continue to exercise their rights to levy, to the Revenue's possible detriment. For local authorities collecting council tax and business rates arrears, whether to instruct the bailiffs is a matter of policy and certainly many local authorities do choose to continue with levies even after bankruptcy.

Administration Orders

Administration Orders are a county court procedure that permits debtors to consolidate all their debts into one total sum that is then administered for them by the court, which distributes affordable payments to all the creditors.

Two conditions must be satisfied in order for a defendant to be able to apply:

► s/he must have at least one county court (or High Court) judgment entered, and,

► have total debts of less than £5000.

If an order has been made, it has a number of effects, such as freezing any interest that may be accruing on the debt, but the most important for our purposes is the consequence for bailiffs.

Tips & Hints

Administration orders make bailiff action for creditors subject to the court agreeing them – rarely will it be worth the creditor making such applications.

Once the Administration Order is made no creditor included on the order can take any action against a debtor except with permission of the court and on such terms as may be imposed.

Notably this also applies to any creditor initially listed on the application form N92, even though the debt was not subsequently included in the order because the court decided that it should be excluded (county courts will often exclude those creditors who have special sanctions to enforce their debts over and above simple court action).

These creditors too will still need permission of the court before being able to enforce even though they are not being paid through the Administration Order. This will particularly affect local taxes and fines which are often excluded after objections by the local authority or magistrates' court.

As in bankruptcy, a landlord may still distrain for rent arrears due after an administration order has been made. The rent recoverable is however restricted to an amount of six month's rent due immediately before the date that the order was made and any other sums due may not be collected by distress - instead the landlord will make a claim in the administration order.

Debt Relief Orders

An individual who is unable to pay his/her debts may apply for a DRO to be made in respect of all unsecured liabilities. Individuals can apply if their total debts are less than £15,000 in total, if they have no significant assets and if their surplus income after paying bills and essentials is less than £50 monthly.

Tips& Hints

Debt relief orders provide considerable protection against bailiff action

When a DRO is made, a moratorium on enforcement comes into effect. The result of this is that, whilst it lasts, the creditor to whom a qualifying debt is owed has no remedy in respect of the debt, and may not commence any action or other legal proceedings against the debtor for the debt, except with the permission of the court and on such terms as the court may impose.

This will prevent all forms of bailiff enforcement. The moratorium normally continues for the period of one year beginning with the start date for the order. At the end of the year, the DRO comes to an end and all the debts are written off.

Conclusions

The key issues to remember from this chapter are:

► local and national codes of practice may supplement and extend the controls over the bailiff and can offer valuable extra protection

► enforcement is largely undertaken by public bodies who have wider duties to ensure proper conduct of their staff and agents. If you feel that an authority or its bailiffs have acted incorrectly, you should complain

► insolvency can protect you against enforcement - but always get expert advice first, because it has negative consequences also

Sample 4
Subject Access Request

(Insert own address)

(Insert date)

(Insert organisation address)

To the company secretary (if contact unknown),

Re: (insert name and current address)

I am writing to make a subject access request under the Data Protection Act 1998 for any personal information you hold about me on paper or computer records (or include specific details about the information you require here).

(Insert any information you think the organisation will need to find your information and to confirm your identity. For example, an account reference number; other organisations may require a document bearing your signature for example your passport or your driving licence).

Please inform me, prior to processing this request, if you require a fee to be paid.

I will look forward to receiving this information within 40 days. If you have any queries or questions then please contact me on (insert phone number/email address).

Yours faithfully,

(Insert own name)

Chapter Four
When the Bailiff Visits

Chapter Contents

This chapter will examine:

Final warnings

Inevitably, the bailiff's call will never come entirely out of the blue. There will have been at least some contact from the creditor before the decision to enforce is made. The purpose of this is both to give warning but also to give you a last opportunity to arrange payment. Most creditors would rather negotiate some term of payment rather than issue enforcement if possible. The nature and amount of warning given will depend on the debt due.

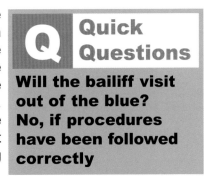

Quick Questions

Will the bailiff visit out of the blue? No, if procedures have been followed correctly

Government agencies who are creditors will all have clear procedures steadily building up from default in payment to enforcement, with clear warnings of what will follow and ample opportunities for you to pay or to challenge the sum claimed to be due (see page 17, chapter 2).

In cases requiring prior court action, there will of course have been plenty of paperwork already and a clear indication of where matters were heading. In addition:

council tax and business rates:
   after getting a liability order, the local authority will ask for personal financial information in an effort to reach a payment arrangement. If this fails, then

the bailiff will call. It is not possible to set aside the liability order once made, so the only option is to negotiate with the local authority (see page 19, chapter 2).

Negotiate with the local authority

The bailiffs should not call, provided no instalments are missed or no other warrant is outstanding

civil court judgments:
generally judgments will be payable forthwith by lump sum unless the defendant applies to pay by instalments. In the county court a warrant cannot be issued until the person liable under the judgment has defaulted on at least one instalment and so long as no previous warrant is outstanding. When a warrant is issued the bailiff will, in either case, give some prior warning.

fines:
upon conviction, the magistrates' court must serve a notice setting out the terms and means of payment; this is a necessary precondition to any enforcement action by the fines officer.

The main exception to all of this is *distress for arrears of rent*. There may be no warning of rent distress. The right of a landlord to distrain exists automatically when property is let. It need not be expressly mentioned in the tenancy agreement or lease - although the right to distrain may be excluded by that agreement.

Rent arrears: there need be no warning of bailiff action. If you have a problem paying, negotiate

The tenant has until the last minute of the day fixed for payments to pay the rent due and distress cannot be levied until the next day. Then, however, the landlord may distrain immediately for all or part of the arrears. If the rent is due on a Sunday, the landlord can distrain on a Monday. The landlord need not demand the rent before distraining unless this is stipulated in the tenancy agreement.

As mentioned in chapter 2 some application to court may be needed first which will of course provide warning. Clearly if it appears unavoidable that a payment will be missed, and the landlord is one likely to enforce promptly (e.g. a commercial landlord of business premises or a smaller local authority) it is wise to pre-empt this risk by warning them of the problem and attempting dialogue.

Initial visits

Most of the fee scales in operation pay bailiffs to make two or three visits to premises without having to levy on goods. In any case, enforcement firms will want to do this to gather information on matters such as the type of property, on the type of door locks and other means of access and on the likelihood of there being goods worth seizing.

Once the visits covered by the fee scales have been made without a levy taking place, the bailiff will clearly consider whether it is worth trying to visit again, based upon what has been found out about the means of the individual.

The National Standard imposes on the bailiff the duty of delivering to the premises a notice to demonstrate that an actual visit has been made. Letters delivered by Royal Mail do not count towards this. It is always worth checking the bailiff's bill in this respect, as there is a considerable body of evidence to suggest that

Do not panic at notices received

many firms charge for visits although they are never actually made - or charge the visit fees for other activities (see chapter 7 later).

The notices posted and delivered at your home will display a nice line in red ink and capital letters, warning of various dire actions including forced entry, removal of goods and committal to prison for non-payment. For many bailiff companies, no progression or logical order is discernible in these; the threats often seem to be random and disconnected from the bailiffs actual activity on the case.

Do not panic because of these notices. Careful reading will often show that they are qualified by phrases such as "if appropriate" or "if necessary". Reading this and later chapters will show when forced entry and removal are real possibilities.

Mostly these notices are not genuine warnings of imminent action but are designed to provoke a response from you.

A levy is improper if outside certain hours

Time of visit

Rules regulate both the day and the hour of a bailiff's call. Visits outside these may be illegal and certainly, if you feel that the time of calling was unreasonable, you should make a complaint and seek an explanation for the time chosen.

What days are allowed?

Distress for rent should not be levied on Sundays or on public holidays like Christmas and Easter. Execution may be levied on a Sunday in an emergency with permission of court and otherwise on any day. Failing to comply with these restrictions will render the levy illegal.

On top of these legal rules, the National Standard recommends that, as a matter of good practice, no form of enforcement should be carried out on Sundays, Bank Holidays, Good Friday or on Christmas Day.

In addition to these restrictions set by law, the National Standard suggests some other days on which a bailiff's call might not be acceptable. Bailiffs are advised to be aware of dates for religious festivals and to consider carefully the appropriateness of enforcement on any day of religious or cultural observance or during any major religious or cultural festival. If, on arriving at your home, the bailiff finds that you are celebrating a particular festival or event, he should not try to levy but should leave and postpone enforcement until another day.

What times are allowed?

Bailiffs levying execution and statutory distraint may levy at any time of day. However, this right may be restricted by the code of practice under which the bailiff operates – the National Standard sets 'reasonable' hours of visiting, which are between 6 am and 9 pm.

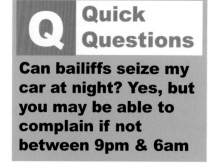

Quick Questions

Can bailiffs seize my car at night? Yes, but you may be able to complain if not between 9pm & 6am

Note, that in levies for fines and road traffic penalties where the car is often the asset seized, visits will usually be at night or early in the morning as it is then that the vehicle is most likely to be found at the house. Where the levy has taken place outside the hours set by the National Standard, it would not be inappropriate to ask why it was felt necessary to come at such an 'unreasonable' time.

There are two exceptions to the above general rule. One is for VAT where the regulations only permit distress between 8 am and 8 pm, though, once started, a levy can continue outside these times.

That said, if the business which is liable for VAT trades partly or wholly outside these times, distress may be made at a convenient hour of opening.

Tips& Hints

Distress for VAT arrears must occur between 8am & 8pm

The other exception to this rule is in distress for rent where a levy should not occur between sunset and sunrise. If the bailiff levies distress for rent at the wrong hour the distress is 'illegal' (for the implications of which see chapter 8) unless you choose to waive the error.

Place of visit

The basic rule is that a person's goods may be seized wherever they are to be found. This could include the following locations.

your home - of course, this is generally the only address the bailiff will have.

your business address - this may be supplied to the bailiff by a creditor where a trade debt is involved or where you are known to be self-employed as a sole trader;

the highway - bailiffs recovering rent arrears for landlords are not entitled to distrain upon goods found on the highway. In all other cases, a levy in the street will be perfectly lawful.

A number of consequences arise from this, all linked to motor vehicles. A person trying to conceal a car from a bailiff cannot simply park it round the corner from home and assume that it is safe and beyond seizure. This is obviously not the case - moreover, the widespread use now by enforcement agencies of ANPR (see page 27, chapter 2 earlier) means that cars may be found almost anywhere they are parked on the road in England and Wales and may be seized there. This makes it far more difficult for a person to conceal a motor vehicle from a bailiff.

The other related issue is to do with the enforcement of road traffic penalties. Many bailiffs' firms now operate in conjunction with the police and they will together conduct operations to check traffic on main roads and pull over those with outstanding road traffic offences, unpaid car tax or unpaid penalty charge notices. It is plainly perfectly legal for such enforcement work to be conducted in the street like this; the main matter for attention will be the charges that are levied on such occasions (see chapter 7 later).

Although bailiffs executing statutory distress may go anywhere in England and Wales, certain limits are placed on other bailiffs' movements.

In execution: the county court bailiff may only operate within that particular court's area.

In distress for rent: the bailiff or landlord can only attend at the rented premises unless goods have been 'fraudulently removed' elsewhere (see page 28, chapter 2 earlier) or the unless you consent to a levy elsewhere.

As stated, the landlord may not levy off the premises in the street. There is an exception to this though where goods are located in the street immediately outside the rented premises, as the courts have decided that a rented property includes half the road outside, so in theory a car parked not only in a drive but immediately outside a house can be seized, whereas one directly opposite in the street or outside a neighbour's house cannot.

A levy at the wrong place could make the distress illegal (see chapter 8)

Taxes: whilst there is no statutory limitation on premises at which distraint may be levied and the warrant permits the bailiff enter any house or premises in order to levy distress, usually bailiffs are only directed by the tax collectors to business premises as there are most likely to be assets there.

Bailiffs' rights of entry

The well-known advice on bailiffs is that you don't have to let them in and that, if you keep the windows and doors shut, they won't be able to gain access to your home. These statements are by and large correct, as the following sections will explain in detail.

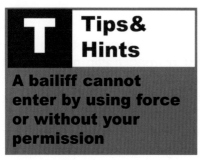

A bailiff cannot enter by using force or without your permission

General principles
The basic rule applying to all bailiffs is that they have a right of entry in order to execute a lawful warrant, but the right may only be exercised if it is done:

- without the use of force; and,

- with the permission of the occupier of the premises.

If entry is made in violation of these two principles, it will be illegal and you will need to consider the remedies described in chapter 8. A criminal offence may also be committed (see also chapter 8).

Case Study As recently as 1998 the Court of Appeal, in the case of *Khazanchi v Faircharm Investments*, confirmed that these principles apply to all initial entries to premises by bailiffs (subject to some exceptions listed later). Nonetheless, what many bailiffs understand by 'forcible' entry is different to what the law intends whilst many bailiffs are wholly unaware of the duty to enter only with permission.

The National Standard imposes further conditions on the bailiff when arriving at a property. If the door is opened by a child, enquiries may be made as to the whereabouts of the parent - if the child appears to be over the age of 12 - otherwise the bailiff must depart immediately. It seems very clear that no valid entry could follow if the door was opened by a minor.

Tips& Hints

A bailiff cannot deal with a child below the age of 12, and only with older children to ask a parent's whereabouts

If you are absent from the premises, a bailiff may endeavour to make enquiries from other occupiers or with the neighbours. The National Standard also demands confidentiality and discreteness in such situations.

Forced entry

When the law prohibits forced entry it makes it illegal to enter premises by a range of means, which include:

► breaking or pushing open the door or window;

► using a locksmith to gain access;

► pushing past a person who is seeking to prevent an entry; or,

► preventing a door being closed by placing a foot in the way.

Most enforcement agents understand that a violent entry is not acceptable;

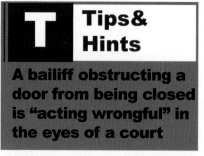
it seems many believe that 'passive' means, such as obstructing the door so it cannot be closed, are not wrongful. The courts are clear, though, that it they are.

Permission to enter

The bailiff acting on a lawful instruction from a court or creditor has the right to come in and, if he arrives at the premises and finds the door or window open or a door closed, but not locked, he may quite properly come in. Failing to secure access is regarded as an implied invitation to enter from the occupier.

If the bailiff is discovered by the occupier immediately after he has entered and is asked to leave, he must leave if he has not actually started the process of levying (that is, listing and securing goods - see chapter 5). The bailiff has no choice about this - his right to remain continues only so long as it has not been expressly cancelled, so if the

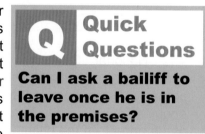
person makes it clear that his presence is no longer welcome, the bailiff's duty is to respect this and to leave.

If a bailiff obtains entry by false pretences, it will be a violation of this principle. If you believe that the bailiff is acting in another capacity, or he asks to come in for another reason (for instance, to use the phone or toilet) - and you grant access on this basis - it will be possible for you to withdraw the permission to be on the premises as soon as the real reason for the visit becomes apparent. In other words, if the bailiff did not want to use the loo but wants to distrain your goods, he can be told to go.

Readers may note that it is, in theory at least, possible to refuse a bailiff entry before he has even crossed the boundary of a property. No less an authority than Lord Scarman suggested in one case that it would be possible to put up a sign on the front gate of a property, forbidding entry to police officers and bailiffs, and this would have to be respected. This curious fact underlines the quite weak rights of entry that bailiffs actually possess.

Premises

Your home is protected from any forced entry. This protection extends to all buildings within the boundary of the premises, i.e. sheds, garages and the like.

Separate, non-domestic premises: private bailiffs levying distress can never break into any premises but there is an exception for execution - see later.

Flats, maisonettes and bedsits: The front door of a flat or bedsit is an outer door and therefore cannot be forced. Thus peaceable entry of the main door of the building still means that the bailiff has yet to effect peaceable entry of your own 'front' door.

Manner of entry

Doors: the bailiff may enter an open door or open an unlocked door. Breaking open a door or gate is trespass. Use of a locksmith to open a door is illegal. If the door is secured shut, it is illegal to force it open, but reasonable force may be used to see if a door is fastened.

Tips& Hints

If a door, window or wall is broken in gaining entry, the entry is illegal

Windows: a bailiff may climb through an open window or skylight and open one wider if necessary but a window pane cannot be broken. Though a bailiff may open a closed but unfastened door he cannot open a closed but un-fastened window. The bailiff cannot open a closed, latched window and the fastening securing a window may not be removed.

Walls: the bailiff may climb over a wall or fence or walk across a garden or yard provided these are not damaged in the process. If the door, window or wall are already broken open, it would seem that the bailiff may enter.

Keys: Use of a landlord's pass key is illegal. It would not matter whether the bailiff found the key or it was provided by a landlord. However, if a key is left in the lock it seems it may be permissible to turn it like a door handle to open the door.

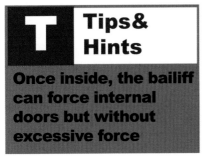

Tips& Hints

Once inside, the bailiff can force internal doors but without excessive force

Internal doors: In contrast to everything said so far, the bailiff may break open any door or cupboard both to find goods or to escape if he is locked in. No demand need be made before forcing each inner door, but this precludes unnecessary use of force - for instance, a door should not be broken if the you offer to open it.

Exceptions

Income taxes: the Inland Revenue collector of taxes may force entry to premises, though some demand for entry should be made first. Use of this power is very rare. The procedure for forcing entry is as follows. The collector must apply to a JP for a warrant which will be granted if the magistrate is satisfied there is a reasonable ground for believing the person is "neglecting or refusing" to pay the income tax that is due.

Beware - force can be used in certain exceptional circumstances

Once issued the collector may only force entry under the warrant during the 'daytime'. The courts have decided that the collector cannot break in without a constable being present, presumably to ensure that there is no breach of the peace.

Magistrates' court fines where the bailiff is enforcing a penalty imposed for a criminal conviction, there is a power to force entry to premises in order to be able to distrain, where this is reasonable and necessary. Since the power was introduced in 2006, it is fair to say that it has only been used sparingly.

It is unlikely the costs of forced entry will be risked for fines enforcement unless the bailiff is sure there are goods to seize

Given this fact, and given that bailiffs may rarely consider it worthwhile risking the expense, readers may wish to stick with the principle that "you don't have to let them in." Although in the case of fines enforcement the risk of force being used must always be borne in mind, a bailiffs' company may only think it worthwhile incurring the cost of a locksmith's attendance where there is a very strong likelihood of distrainable goods being found which would justify the forced entry.

Separate or non-domestic premises (e.g. a workshop or warehouse) may be entered forcibly but only in cases of execution of civil court judgments. This right does not apply if the non-domestic premises are connected to a dwelling, even though they may have separate entrances and no communicating doors - for instance a flat over a shop. The bailiffs should make enquiry as to the presence of goods first, otherwise they risk trespassing.

Strangers' premises may be entered forcibly by a landlord with a police officer if an oath has been sworn before magistrates to the effect that there are grounds for believing goods have been fraudulently removed there (see page 28, chapter 2).

Bailiffs - The Law and Your Rights

The HCEO may also break into a third party's house if goods have been taken there to avoid execution. Demand for entry should be made first. Also a bailiff may enter such premises peaceably to search for goods but will be a trespasser if either no goods are found or if inner doors are forced in the process.

Re-entry may be forced after a previous, lawful levy (see chapter 6 for details). Readers should be beware of a fairly common practice by bailiffs: some will assert that, under an existing levy, they are entitled to force entry so as to be able to conduct a levy for a debt which has been subsequently been passed to them for collection. This is wrong and is a violation of the right of forced re-entry.

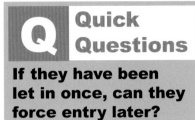

Quick Questions

If they have been let in once, can they force entry later?

Tips & Hints

Bailiffs must secure a property once they leave, or face a claim for any losses incurred

When leaving a property which has been entered by force the bailiff should leave it in a secure condition. The bailiff could face a court claim for any losses arising from a failure to do this (see chapter 8).

Police involvement

A common threat that readers will encounter is that of the police being called to attend at (and implicitly to assist in) the bailiff's entry. The widespread reference to these powers in bailiffs' correspondence can give a distorted or misleading impression of what they may do. A police officer certainly may be asked by either party to attend - either before or during a levy or forced entry - but only if a threat of violence can be shown to be anticipated or if one occurs.

The officer's presence would be to prevent a breach of the peace and definitely not to assist in the seizure. A breach of the peace may be defined as a situation when and where:

Quick Questions

Can the bailiff call the police to help them?

► harm is actually done or is likely to be done to a person whether by the conduct of the person against whom the breach is alleged or by someone provoking that breach;

► harm is actually done or is likely to be done to a person's property in his presence, provided that the natural consequences of such harm is likely to be a violent retaliation; or,

► a person is genuinely in fear of harm to him/herself or property in their presence as a result of an assault.

The police may enter any premises if necessary in the course of their duty to prevent breaches of the peace, though they will need to show any entry was reasonably necessary in the circumstances.

Q Quick Questions

Would the police act against a bailiff?

They can arrest the person who commits, or who they reasonably believe will commit, a breach of the peace. This could be either you or the bailiff, though it has recently been emphasised that a bailiff acting lawfully whilst enforcing a warrant will seldom be regarded as being in breach of the peace, whilst those resisting a lawful levy with threats of violence will be guilty of breaching the peace.

The involvement of the police can only be justified by the bailiff if it can be shown that it was necessary because of the use of or threats of resistance or of violence, or because similar circumstances were met on a previous visit. In other cases (the majority) reference to the police is generally an effort to increase pressure upon you to allow the bailiff entry.

As already seen, entry may be legally refused and no offence is committed. Sadly, on those occasions when the police are asked to attend, they often do seem to 'side with' the bailiff and add to the pressure on the occupier to permit entry against his/ her will. Readers may need considerable resolve to resist this. Inviting the police officers in to read this book, or to check with someone senior at their station, may be an option!

Resistance

If a wrongful entry is discovered it is permissible for a person to resist it (within limits). However, ejecting a bailiff who has entered legally can lead to forced re-entry by the bailiff and may be a criminal offence. The courts have sanctioned the use of reasonable force to resist entry by bailiffs in three different contexts:

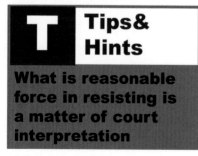

T **Tips& Hints**

What is reasonable force in resisting is a matter of court interpretation

where the bailiff's status was not disclosed; where the bailiff forces entry, and where the bailiff ignores a request not to enter.

However, there is a considerable problem with the use of self help to resist illegal entry. 'Reasonable force' may be employed - but what is reasonable? The courts seem to have interpreted the term quite generously in favour of the occupier, but the risks inherent in the remedy are considerable and it is strongly recommended to readers that taking the law into your own hands in this way is avoided. If a remedy is required, urgent court action as described in chapter 8 is far preferable.

Entry: Conclusions

If entry can't be gained at all, the bailiff is unlikely to give up on the first visit. Notice of their attendance will be left and further visits will be made at different times on different days. Discrete enquiries may also be made from neighbours as to person's presence or movements.

Despite all the hurdles and potential problems, it must be accepted that entry is actually achieved in a very large number of cases. Regardless of the technicalities, gaining entry is as much to do with psychology as law and skilled bailiffs will play on a person's shame of their financial situation to enable them to get in. It may take considerable will power to resist a man on the doorstep in such circumstances.

Tips& Hints

Entry is not the be-all-and-end all

To recap, bailiffs' entry to premises will be rendered unlawful by:

▶ the use of force;

▶ being misleading or lying about their identity or purpose; or,

▶ gaining access when only a child or an adult without authority is present on the premises.

However, if an entry is illegal because it violates one of the principles listed, it may be trespass and then you will have the remedies described in chapter 8.

Identification

The basic principle is that you should always be entitled to know who is calling at your home and why. The bailiff should be able to produce some sort of identification - possibly for himself personally and certainly to show who he is acting for and what he is collecting. This gives you a last chance to pay.

The bailiff does not have to have the warrant personally upon him/herself, as long as it is accessible nearby in the car or van. A warrant held that the firm's head office is not acceptable (but see fines below). If you ask to see the warrant and it is not available, it can render anything done after that point unlawful and invalid (see chapter 8).

Over and above these minimum requirements, for certain debts special rules are laid down.

► Fines: a **bailiff** collecting a fine must explain exactly why he has called and the consequences of the visit. The bailiff should show you his warrant and his authorisation to act for the magistrates court; if the warrant is not immediately available when it is asked for arrangements should be made for it to be inspected.

► Road traffic penalties: the bailiff must show his warrant from the traffic authority and also produce his county court certificate if asked (see chapter 8).

► Rent: the bailiff must show his warrant from the landlord and also produce his county court certificate if asked (see chapter 8).

Conclusions

The important points to remember are:

► there will normally be some warning - don't ignore it!

► most bailiffs can go to any premises you own at any time

► they have a right to enter, but not with force - i.e. you can refuse

► remember though, if they can't get in, the bailiffs may still seize goods outside

► you are entitled to ask for identification and other details

► any breach of these general rules may make the visit illegal

Checklist of bailiffs' entry rights

Type of bailiff	Time of entry	Place of entry	First entry	Return to Remove
County court/ High Court	Any time (not usually Sundays)	Anywhere in area of county court's jurisdiction	Home-peaceable Business-force may be used	Forced if necessary (though warning should be given before return)
Income tax	Any time	Anywhere in England & Wales	Forced if necessary	As above
VAT	8am- 8pm, unless firm trades at other times Any day	Anywhere	Peaceable at all premises	As above
Fines	Any time	Anywhere	May be forced as a 'last resort'; bailiffs may use "reasonable force, if necessary..."	As above
Other statutory distraint - CSM/ local taxes etc.	Any time	Anywhere	Peaceable at all premises	As above
Distress for rent	Between sunrise & sunset; not Sundays	Only at rented premises	As above	As above

Chapter Five
The Levy Process

Chapter Contents

This chapter will examine:

Introduction

Before examining the process of levying in detail, it is worthwhile observing that bailiffs are not really interested in taking and selling most goods. What is valuable to them is the threat to you of your goods being removed and sold rather than the value of the goods themselves. It is the risk of losing possessions which makes people pay, along with the wish to avoid the stress and embarrassment of a bailiff's visit.

Tips& Hints

Beware: most goods are of less value than your car

Furthermore, most second hand household items are of limited value and will not sell at auction for very much. Some items, such as electrical goods, although expensive to buy, are difficult to sell at auction because of rules on their safety. As a result, even though a house may be emptied of all of its contents, the debt and costs may still not be cleared.

Because of the matters discussed above, many bailiffs' firms would prefer to seize motor vehicles if they are available. They retain their value much better than household chattels and are also much more accessible. There is, however, a considerable risk of such a levy being 'excessive' (see chapter 8) unless the bailiff has taken care to establish that there was genuinely nothing else of sufficient value in the house which might have been seized instead.

Levying

The 'levy' is the key stage of the enforcement procedure. It is essential for the bailiff to get this stage right, or else all successive stages will be placed in jeopardy. Without a valid levy, there will be no right to re-enter, remove or sell.

However, it is a technical and complex process that is often ill-understood and mistakes often occur. Equally, corners are often cut in order to save time and money.

There are three stages to the process of levying:

► first entry to the premises: as described in the last chapter;

► seizure of the goods: by taking an inventory. This is the process of identifying the goods which will cover the debt and costs outstanding; and,

► impounding of the goods: the process of placing them in 'legal custody' so that they are protected from interference and so that the bailiff will later be entitled to remove and sell them.

Tips& Hints

Entry may not be required if there are goods of sufficient value outside

You should note that, when visiting a person's home, a bailiff does not have to get inside a house if there are adequate goods outside. A car or garden equipment might be levied without any need to consider furniture. This is perfectly lawful; the only condition is that the bailiff must still provide you with all the necessary documents to support the levy (see page 74 below).

Seizure

The act of seizure of a debtor's goods is the process of selecting, valuing and recording items necessary to cover the debt and costs. There are two forms of seizure:

actual:
as the name suggests this will involve the bailiff actually seeing, even touching, the goods that are to be seized and listed for sale. It may well be coupled with a clear declaration of the bailiff's intention

constructive
this form of seizure is far harder to define. The bailiff's intentions may be inferred from his actions, e.g. looking through a window, walking round

premises, making and presenting a written notice of the goods being seized or by some means preventing the removal of certain goods. Physical contact is not essential provided that something has been done to intimate seizure has been made. The method used in most cases is the making of an inventory.

A bailiff is not necessarily entitled to all the goods on the premises and has to select sufficient to cover the debt and costs whilst ensuring this is not excessive. This involves some process of selection before seizure and where this fails to happen the levy may be open to challenge. A claim on an inventory to "all goods" on the premises could well be excessive (see page 85 below).

Tips & Hints

A bailiff is not entitled to all your goods.

Even though a valid seizure may have occurred, it must be stressed that the levy process is not yet complete. Seizure gives the bailiff immediate control of the goods, but they must now be impounded for the seizure to have any effect on you and for the bailiff to retain control.

A person may be guilty of criminal contempt if s/he obstructs a civil court bailiff in the execution of their duty. Obstruction includes assault and retaking seized goods (also termed 'rescue'). The bailiff can arrest the person and the court may commit or fine the offender. It would be a defence for you to say that you honestly, but mistakenly, believed the victim was not a court officer or was not acting in execution of his duty. Rescue is also wrongful in other forms of seizure of goods, but is virtually never prosecuted nowadays.

Impounding

Impounding is essential in order to change the status of the seized goods. A bailiff may walk round a property and make a list of goods that he has 'seized', but this alone counts for little. For the bailiff to have the power to return later, break into the premises, remove the goods on the inventory and sell them, he must acquire some legal control over them. This is done by impounding.

Technically, when the goods are impounded they are said to be placed in the 'custody of the law' and interference with them by you or any one else will be the offence of 'poundbreach' (see page 76 below).

There are a number of different forms of impounding available for bailiffs to use, depending upon the debt which they are enforcing. The most common are discussed in the following sections.

Immediate Removal

The bailiff takes away the selected goods to a store room at the end of the first visit. In fact, this method is rarely used because of the expense and trouble involved. Nevertheless, goods in shops or factories may be removed immediately if the bailiff feels that the firm cannot settle the debt and there is a risk of assets being disposed of, removed or hidden. This is especially likely to be the case if a previous possession agreement was breached.

Securing on the premises

Securing in a room or other location on the premises is permissible in distress for rent only but is seldom used by landlords. Note though it is not permissible for a bailiff levying any other form of distraint or execution to lock up goods in a room on the premises.

Tips & Hints

The bailiff cannot lock you out of part or all of your property to seize goods

Further, it is illegal for any bailiff to impound goods by locking up the entire premises, so completely excluding the occupier. This is tantamount to eviction and there is no power to do this. The warrant licences the bailiff to seize goods, not to seize a property, and to endeavour to take exclusive possession of premises in this way is trespass (for which see chapter 8).

Close possession

A bailiff can be left guarding the goods as 'possession man'. Today the cost and staffing problems associated with close possession means that it is virtually never used.

Quick Questions

Is clamping legal as a way to seize goods?

Clamping

Clamping is frequently used by bailiffs when levying upon motor vehicles. That said, its use for the majority of debts is highly questionable. It is sanctioned by the legislation as a means of impounding in distress for rent (it is a way of securing on the premises), in county court execution and in magistrates' courts (because a specific clamping order may be issued for the enforcement of a fine).

In all other cases, there is no clear authority for using the procedure to be found in the legislation and it would therefore appear to be a trespass against the vehicle which has been clamped. It does not matter whether the clamp is applied as a long-term form of impounding or if it is a temporary measure until a tow truck arrives - either way the bailiff has immobilised the vehicle without lawful authority.

If clamping is a trespass, your remedies are exactly as with a trespass to land by an illegal entry as described in the previous chapter: you may issue a county court claim for damages or you may take self-help action to release the vehicle from its immobilisation (see chapter 8).

You may take self-help action to remove the clamp yourself but be careful

Self-help is attractive because it is immediate and gets the car back on the road; there are, however, several problems with this course of action.

▶ although you may be entitled to release the car from the clamp, this must be done without damaging the clamp in any way. Some clamps may be released by letting down tyres, many cannot. To damage the clamp might lead (rightly or wrongly) to accusations of criminal damage

▶ secondly, the victim of the trespass may be entitled to free the car from the clamp, but s/he is not entitled to keep the clamp. The problem therefore is to restore it to the bailiff; if this is not done directly and promptly, a threat of prosecution for theft of the clamp might be made

▶ the bailiff may try to charge you for damage to or loss of the clamp by adding extra fees onto those allowed for the levy. Such fees are not permitted by the fee scales (see chapter 7) and the bailiff can only get compensation by issuing a county court claim. Of course, a counterclaim for trespass by immobilising your vehicle might be your response (!)

▶ you may be accused of interference with impounded goods (see section 6 later). Such accusations will generally be mistaken - unless the clamping was valid, say for rent or under a magistrates order.

Finally, note that the case of *Culligan v Simkin & Marstons Group* (2009) confirmed that, when clamping is used, it should be treated as a form of impounding, for which a levy fee is chargeable, rather than part of the process of removal, for which different fees are charged (see chapter 6).

Marking the goods

In the magistrates' court, the Criminal Procedure Rules require that a bailiff clearly mark any goods seized during a levy. This constitutes impounding on the premises and is the method to be used instead of any of the others mentioned here. What form this mark will take exactly is not laid down, but it is clear that walking possession and clamping will not be valid without it.

Walking possession

This is the form of possession or impounding taken almost exclusively nowadays. Walking possession is a process whereby a person agrees (usually in writing) that the goods will remain in his/her premises, subject to the bailiffs' ongoing claim and to their right to return and remove them for sale and also subject to payment of a daily fee to the bailiff

(though this fee may be small and its duration limited).

For you the inconvenience of losing the use of items is avoided. For the bailiff the inconvenience of leaving a bailiff or removing goods is overcome. Both parties benefit from the breathing space during which arrangements to pay can be explored.

A simple definition of walking possession, bearing in mind the other possible forms of impounding, may be to say that the person who signs is being appointed as 'possession man' by the bailiff, as an agent of the bailiff guarding his/her own goods on behalf of the bailiff.

Any 'responsible' person on the premises, including the spouse, partner, employee or adult relative of the indebted individual, can in most cases make the agreement. Your authority or consent is not necessary. "Responsible" may be defined as being regularly or permanently at the premises and understanding and being able to pass on the consequences of walking possession. Individuals only temporarily present in the property at the time the bailiff calls are not suitable.

The person who signs a walking possession agreement should understand that the goods should not be moved by anyone else. They must be able to explain the existence of the impounding to the person in debt and others (such as other bailiffs who may call). The would be required to stop items being removed and should tell the bailiff if they are.

In local tax legislation stricter requirements are laid down in the fee scales. If the statutory walking possession fee is to be charged, the only acceptable signatory is the debtor named on the liability order, and s/he must sign at the time of the levy. If the debtor does not sign at the right time, no possession charges may be made.

Children will not be able to make such agreements.

It is likely that it will not be acceptable to make an arrangement with a person whose first language is not English or who does not have the mental capacity to understand what they are signing.

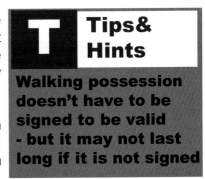

Tips& Hints

Walking possession doesn't have to be signed to be valid - but it may not last long if it is not signed

If the wrong person signs a walking possession agreement, the levy may fail (see page 81 later). You do not have to be at home for a bailiff to be entitled to enter and seize goods, but as your signature is likely to be needed on documentation so in practice the bailiff will prefer you to be there.

The courts have suggested that there are two forms of walking possession:

by signed agreement

normally this will be the form encountered. The bailiff will be keen to get a signed agreement so that his position is clarified and so that he may add on charges for possession. It is likely that pressure will be applied to get your signature, such as the threat of immediate removal. Given the relatively low fees involved, and the fact that it buys time to raise money or get advice, there seems little to be gained by not signing a walking possession agreement

an implied or verbal agreement

walking possession without any written agreement may be implied as having been made in situations where a person acknowledges, or at least cannot deny, that seizure has occurred and that the bailiff has laid claim to certain goods. This can be described as a form of walking possession, as the circumstances of the impounding will be the same: the bailiff is absent from the property, leaving the goods with the indebted person. The courts have decided that impounding has occurred, in the absence of a written possession agreement, where:

▶ you had notice of the bailiff's purpose;

▶ an inventory is taken;

▶ you received notice of impounding (and seizure); and/ or,

▶ you assented to the bailiff taking of possession.

However, as this form of possession is by its nature neither agreed in writing nor physically apparent, regular steps must be taken by the bailiff to ensure that the possession is continued, otherwise it will soon be treated as 'abandoned' - see page 81 later.

These regular steps may be return visits to the property, letters, texts or phone calls. If these steps are not taken, either to acquire or retain possession, you may be able to challenge any later threat to remove and sell. To put such a threat into effect could be trespass by the bailiff (see chapter 8 and 'failed levies' later).

Notices of seizure & inventories

Having concluded the process of seizure and impounding the bailiff will complete the levy by commonly leaving at the property, or with the occupier, a notice of seizure which confirms what has occurred.

Notices will commonly include the following information:

▶ the debt due and costs incurred so far (including a copy of the statutory scale of charges);

▶ an inventory of the goods seized (see later), and;

▶ often, a walking possession agreement. Though strictly speaking this is a separate document, it is often incorporated in to the notice of seizure for convenience.

Other information may also be required to be left by statute, such as a copy of the relevant regulations, and notice of any rights to appeal, interplead or replevy, plus details of the bailiff's certificate, if it is a rent, local tax or road traffic levy (see chapter 8 for details of this).

Where a notice is mandatory, failure to provide one or provision of an inadequate notice will make the distress irregular (see chapter 8). Even though this information may not be required, it is common for most bailiffs to supply it anyway. Often readers will find that all these documents are compressed into one or two sides of A4. Inevitably, much of the information will be in extremely small print as a result!

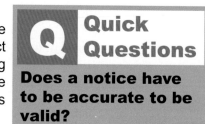

Certain errors on notices will not invalidate them - a wrongly named debtor, or an incorrect date the debt fell due or by not including the date at all. A notice does not have to be presented personally to the debtor in distress for rent or local taxes.

Quick Questions

Does a notice have to be accurate to be valid?

The form of inventories

Case law has established that where an inventory is supplied, it must make it clear what goods have been seized. A notice should either:

▶ list and identify each item seized. Ideally, this should comprise the make, model and even serial number of each chattel listed. Alternatively, a reasonably precise description should be given. Phrases such as 'a collection of DVDs' are not acceptable; or

Tips & Hints

An inventory should be a detailed list

▶ state that all goods on the premises have been seized. The courts have said that this is permissible, if extremely unsatisfactory. The procedure is not only unprofessional, it is also potentially excessive (see chapter 8). For that reason, bailiffs have been discouraged from using it unless it is genuinely applicable because a very large debt is being enforced.

However, either of the above forms of inventory fulfils the basic function of an inventory, which is to inform all those who need to know exactly what has been seized. The inventory is essential to the following parties:

▶ the bailiff and the creditor, so that they can tell whether any items have been removed and so that they know what they are entitled to sell if you still fail to pay;

▶ to indebted individuals, so that they are able to dispute the seizure of any items which they consider should be exempt and so they may inform third parties who might wish to make a claim to any of the goods;

▶ to any third party who might claim ownership of goods and might wish to start court proceedings to protect their interests; and,

▶ to any other bailiffs who may call at the property with the intention of seizing goods. Items which have already been levied upon cannot be levied on again.

Tips & Hints

You can challenge the bailiff if he tries to remove goods not listed on his levy – but beware, he may take them anyway leaving you to go to court

An inventory which is too vague to identify the items impounded precisely will not be lawful. Accordingly, the courts have decided that inventories which claim to seize "all necessary goods", "all goods sufficient to cover the debt" or "all goods except those exempt by law" are too vague to be legally effective and are therefore invalid.

Surprisingly, perhaps, some large bailiffs' firms still use inventories which include this sort of wording. Such levies should be challenged. The bailiff will only ever be entitled to remove the items specifically identified and will not be able to rely on the 'catch-all' phrase to remove other goods at a later date.

It seems that part of the motivation for using these kinds of terms on inventories is in order to cut corners on levying. If a bailiff can claim to have levied by noting down just a couple of items after a chat on the doorstep, without the necessity of entering and inspecting the house thoroughly, he can conduct far more levies during a day. If you subsequently do not pay, the bailiff would return to remove but at that stage would rely on the 'catch-all' phrase to take many more items than were actually identified.

Interference with impounded goods

There are, in theory, two separate wrongful acts that you can commit: rescue and poundbreach. The latter is most likely to occur, though the offences are both often referred to simply as 'rescue.' Each is both an offence for which you may be prosecuted and a civil wrong for which the creditor or bailiff may claim damages.

It would be a defence for you to say that the bailiff had seized goods illegally.

Rescue is interference with goods which have been seized but not yet impounded. Because the two stages of the levy process are effectively merged now, it is going to be rare that an opportunity for rescue arises today.

Poundbreach is interference with impounded goods and is the offence most likely to be committed in these days of walking possession agreements. Such interference is an offence, whether or not there is a breach of the peace. The offender can be prosecuted and on conviction the sentence may be committal for an unlimited period or a fine of an unlimited amount, though based on the guilty person's means and the gravity of the offence.

Such a prosecution is highly unlikely to occur, but there are two specific criminal remedies which are more likely to arise. These are:

county court execution
    section 92 of the County Courts Act 1984 states that any person rescuing

seized goods is liable to up to a month's imprisonment and/or a fine up to £2500. You may be arrested and brought before a judge by the bailiff. Arrest will either be on the spot if you are caught by the bailiff - though you should be given full details of the allegations against you and given an opportunity to prepare a defence, seek legal advice and apply for legal aid. Alternatively proceedings may begin following a claim form from the court.

Tips& Hints

Criminal offences are possible for interfering with impounded goods.

Tips& Hints

Don't remove the mark or remove the goods in magistrates' court cases

magistrates' court
if the bailiff levies upon household goods, they cannot be removed from the house before the day of the sale without your written consent but must instead be impounded with a mark. It is an offence, punishable by fine, to remove the goods or to remove or deface the mark.

There is also a general civil remedy for poundbreach, which is for the creditor to issue a claim for damages.

There are also specific civil remedies for different debts:

Distress for rent
Landlords may claim a penalty of treble damages for both rescue and poundbreach. The basis upon which the damages are calculated is the value of the goods seized. The penalty is recoverable by a claim in the county court by the landlord; and,

Quick Questions

Can the creditor claim damages for poundbreach?

VAT
Under the VAT Act 1994 there is a civil penalty for breach of any walking possession agreement. Fifty percent of the VAT due is simply added onto the existing debt. You will not be liable if you can convince the Commissioners or, on appeal, a VAT Tribunal, that there is a reasonable excuse for the breach. Lack of funds is not regarded as a reasonable excuse.

Naturally in such instances where an offence is alleged, arguments can arise as to whether poundbreach or rescue have indeed occurred and these will in turn involve questions as to whether impounded goods have been abandoned or were properly impounded in the first place.

There will be no abandonment, and therefore an offence will have been committed, where possession is adequately retained or the bailiffs intend to retain it. However no offence is committed by a person where the goods were never effectively seized or impounded, where the claim to possession has lapsed (see section 7 later) or where an innocent third party removed goods, unaware that they are subject to **walking possession**.

For example, it should not treated as poundbreach if another member of a family has moved goods or a hire or HP company has recovered its property. A careful examination of the circumstances of the case may be necessary, considering what documents have been left and what steps were taken.

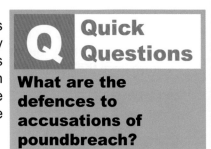

Q Quick Questions

What are the defences to accusations of poundbreach?

Failed levies

As already stated, for a valid levy to have been made both seizure and impounding must occur. To judge whether a bailiff has achieved this, readers should remember the basic rule - a bailiff cannot claim to have legal possession of goods if he was never in the position to have taken physical possession of them.

As a result, as the High Court famously explained in the case of *Evans v South Ribble Borough Council* [1993], a bailiff cannot claim to have levied upon household goods if he has never even managed to enter the premises but merely looked through a window and listed items.

T Tips& Hints

"Abandoned" goods cannot be removed by the bailiff

If the bailiff fails to obtain or to maintain possession of the goods, they are then regarded as having been 'abandoned', i.e. by failing to remain adequately in possession or by delaying his return the bailiff loses any right to return and remove them.

Any sort of agreement or arrangement with you is likely to be evidence of impounding contrary to a claim of abandonment - so if the bailiff can show some sort of walking possession, as a result of which you are making regular payments, his claim to the goods will persist. The result of proving abandonment is that any return and removal by the bailiff would be illegal (see chapter 8).

There are several ways in which bailiffs can fail to complete the process of levying adequately, thus losing their clients' rights to get paid and their own rights to make charges. The most common mistakes are listed in the following paragraphs.

Bailiffs - The Law and Your Rights

Wrong place & time

A possession agreement must be made at the correct stage in the levy process and in the correct circumstances in order to be valid. Thus the following agreements will be vulnerable to challenge by you as there will have been no levy:

those posted to you

an 'agreement' must by definition be between two parties, and should be made at the time of seizure. A partially completed 'walking possession' agreement merely posted to you cannot logically be of any validity as no document signed by one party alone - the bailiff - can constitute an agreement binding on the another - nor has there been an entry to the premises.

A walking possession agreement that is only posted to you will not be valid

Even if you subsequently sign and return it, as is commonly requested, you are not waiving any fault with it or accepting the agreement. Signing the agreement retrospectively will not bar you from any subsequent objection to its legality as one cannot, by one's actions, be deprived of one's rights in ignorance of what they are.

It is clear that a valid agreement must follow a legal entry and levy and that paperwork dropped through the door for signature and return is unacceptable and ineffective. In such cases you may thus continue to deal with goods as you wish as they are not in the custody of the law and cannot be until the bailiff has at least entered the property. Equally no walking possession fee may be charged.

those made off your premises

'walking possession agreements' signed at an office - or anywhere else (for example, in the bailiff's car or van) - without entry or even visits to premises are, by the same token, void.

An entry is required to make a levy on household goods legal

No written agreement & time elapsed

As seen in chapter 4, if it is not possible to persuade the person to sign the bailiff may still manage to impound the goods by an oral agreement. Charges cannot be made for an oral agreement in most cases and, more seriously, the bailiff's rights will be quite short lived.

As explained, if steps are not taken to keep the possession in existence - for example, by follow up visits, letters or phone calls, or of course prompt removal, within a relatively short time the bailiff's rights will be lost. The goods are then 'abandoned' (see earlier) and the seizure process will have to be commenced again from the start.

No agreement

If no agreement is made at all, either written or oral, the bailiff can leave notice on the premises that seizure has occurred and this will operate as a sort of walking possession to adequately impound the goods - but only for a very brief period.

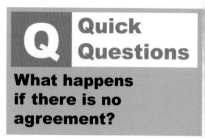

Quick Questions

What happens if there is no agreement?

The notice and your presence during the seizure will be enough for the bailiff to have asserted his legal rights and for you to understand what was intended. However, the right to force re-entry and remove will be extremely transitory and soon lost unless the levy is very quickly followed up. Of course, no charges can be made for possession in this situation.

In this and the previous situation, matters will be different if you start to pay the debt off by instalments as a result of the bailiff's visit. Each time you pay you are acknowledging and renewing the fact of a valid impounding. Weekly or monthly payments therefore keep extending the bailiff's possession and postponing the point at which you could feasibly claim abandonment.

No levy made

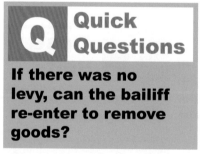

Quick Questions

If there was no levy, can the bailiff re-enter to remove goods?

It quite often happens that a bailiff gains access to premises but does not conduct a levy once inside. Whilst a discussion may have taken place with you about terms of repayment of the debt, there was no actual listing of goods or taking of possession. If these steps are not taken, the mere fact of entry into a house does not constitute a levy. The bailiff will still be at square one and will have no grounds for claiming a right to force re-entry or to remove or sell goods. A further peaceable entry and levy would have to be made.

A new warrant or liability order

It is possible for a bailiff to levy for several debts all at once, something which is quite commonly seen for council tax or road traffic penalties. However, if the same creditor later sends a further instruction to the bailiff, it is not possible to include this debt in an existing levy and walking possession agreement. If a new warrant is received, it will have to be enforced afresh from the start.

Signed walking possession and time elapsed

Even if a perfectly valid walking possession agreement has been made, its main purpose is to secure the creditor's claim to the goods whilst the debt is cleared by instalment payments.

Accordingly, if payments eventually lapse under an agreement after a while, the bailiff should quite promptly follow the matter up. If no payments have been made for several months, and no action has been taken, a point must come where even a signed possession agreement is abandoned.

Summary - invalid levies

Over the last few decades there has been a persistent practice of bailiffs trying to cut corners and save time and money by finding quick and simple ways of levying. These have included the following:

no entry
claims to have levied upon household goods by looking through a window

on doorstep
claims to have levied upon household goods after a conversation with you on the doorstep of the premises, without any entry to the home

off the premises
taking an inventory of goods and making a possession agreement following contact with you at the bailiff's office or elsewhere

'drive-by levies'
the practice of listing car registration numbers following a cursory inspection of the premises from outside and whilst merely driving past. Often these levies are only revealed by getting a copy of the bailiff's bill. You will find you have been charged for a levy you knew nothing about. On enquiry, you will find a car you know nothing about has been seized

two stage levies
some firms have tried to rely on the 'catch-all' phrase at the end of their inventory to save time on the first stage of their levy process. Only one or two items may be formally seized and listed, but the inventory lays claim to having seized everything else in the property.

This means that, if payment arrangements break down, the bailiffs will then aim to return and conduct a thorough search and process of selection within your home. As was stated on page 75 above, the courts have condemned these forms of inventory. All the bailiff will be entitled to remove at the second stage will be the specific items listed at the first stage.

The claim on the inventory to "all other goods necessary" will not have validly impounded anything at all. Only the clearly identified goods will have been effectively impounded and the case law is very clear that the bailiff only gets one chance at getting the levy right and cannot add on other items later.

None of these methods of levying satisfy the basic principles of a valid levy. You should always examine the circumstances of a levy, bearing the following key principles in mind. It is incumbent on the bailiff to inspect the property and search for goods in order to ascertain what is available, what it is worth and whether or not it belongs to you. Household goods can only be seized after an actual entry to the house: the bailiff can only claim to have successfully taken possession if, at the time of the levy, s/he was in a position to physically remove the items if another means of possession was not possible.

In summary, if a levy is invalid or if there has been abandonment, any attempt to sell, remove or collect charges for any of these will be illegal (see chapter 8 for remedies).

Consequences of a failed levy

Even though it may be possible to argue that a levy has been defective either because of the manner of entry, the means of impounding or the contents of the inventory, this is only the end of the bailiff's progress to that point. It does not mean that he cannot try again and it certainly does not mean that the debt has been written off.

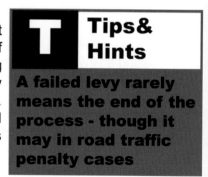

Tips & Hints

A failed levy rarely means the end of the process - though it may in road traffic penalty cases

If the warrant or liability order is returned to the creditor, whether because the bailiff has been unable to levy successfully or has found no goods of any value, the creditor will have other means of recovery available. In all cases the relevant legislation gives creditors a range of means of recovery which they can try and in most cases the account will simply move on to the next stage of the process - for example, for fines or council tax an application for committal to prison may well follow.

The only regular exception to this is road traffic penalties. Although the court rules give local authorities a range of other measures they can try in the county

Bailiffs - The Law and Your Rights

court, this is very rarely done and a failure by the bailiff may, to all intents and purposes, mean that the debt has been written off.

Prior claims

Another factor for the bailiff to take into account during a levy are any prior claims to which you may be liable. As will be seen, there may be little to be gained directly by raising such issues, other than to disrupt the levy. However, it may be that the bailiff abandons a levy rather than have to deal with the prior claimants. The main ones are the Crown and landlords seeking rent arrears.

Crown priority

It is a long established principle that the Crown is entitled to priority in recovery proceedings, whether it is enforcing by execution or by distress. If a government department seeks to levy and finds a landlord or other creditor already in possession, it may proceed as its debt takes precedence. This cannot occur if the goods seized under the earlier levy have been sold, for then the goods no longer belong to the debtor.

Landlord's claims

Landlords are given priority rights to claim payment for arrears of rent due under a current tenancy from any bailiff levying execution for judgments and road traffic penalties.

The bailiff is under no liability to enquire as to the existence of rent arrears, but if notice of a claim is received the bailiff should investigate it. When a claim is received the county court or road traffic bailiff should then also levy for the rent and costs. Upon sale, the bailiff will satisfy

> **T Tips & Hints**
>
> **Prior claims for rent arrears are no protection – two sets of bailiffs may have to agree between them to levy once and settle both debts after.**

firstly the costs of the sale, then the landlord's claim. A similar procedure is followed by the High Court enforcement officer.

What can and can't be seized

The final important matter to consider in this chapter is what the bailiff can actually levy upon. Bailiffs can normally seize both your goods and money (including banknotes and cheques). All the same, a large number of categories of asset are exempt, as will be described in the following sections.

If any exempt goods are seized, the onus of proof is on you initially to show that they are exempt because they fall into any particular category or below any financial limit.

The Levy Process

However, the courts have also held that bailiffs have a duty of care that they must exercise when seizing goods. They must act with discernment and judgment.

If, during an actual levy, the bailiffs receive a reasonable and believable claim that certain goods do not belong to you or should be exempted, they must act with due caution and circumspection and should try to seize other items in preference if possible. If they do not act in this manner, an illegal levy may have occurred (see chapter 8).

Tips & Hints

A bailiff should no seize goods that do not belong to the debtor

Very recently this duty of the bailiff was re-emphasised by the High Court in the case of *Huntress Search v Canapeum Ltd & DSI Foods* [2010]. A HCEO called at a different address to the one on the writ, refused to inspect documents showing that DSI Foods was owner of the goods in question having bought them off Canapeum Ltd when it went into liquidation, refused to speak to the administrator of the insolvent company Canapeum and generally acted in what the Court called a high-handed and unprofessional manner. This underlines the fact that the bailiff has to take great care to ensure that the goods being seized genuinely are yours.

The categories of seizable and exempt goods are described in the paragraphs that follow. Distress for rent is dealt with separately at page 94 because of its unique nature. If any of these rules are breached, an action for wrongful interference or replevin may be possible (see chapter 8).

Items in use
One very old exemption is for items being used personally by an individual or items of clothing or jewellery actually being worn. These cannot be seized simply because to try to do so would very likely give rise to a breach of the peace.

Tips & Hints

Bailiffs cannot seize what you are wearing: you can wear jewellery or other clothing you wish to protect

Valuable goods only
The bailiff can only seize property that can be sold. Consequently, items that cannot be sold - such as deeds, personal papers or effects - should not be the subject of a levy. Items of no value or minimal value should also not be seized (e.g. old or broken possessions).

The sort of goods typically worth seizing are business assets, cars, high quality domestic furniture, garden equipment and antique and 'art' items. These will be seized based on a valuation of their sale price at auction.

It is difficult to sell many second hand goods by auction because of controls, such as Consumer Protection Act 1987, over the electrical safety of audio visual and white goods, the fireproofing of furniture and the safety of children's items. Personal jewellery and effects are also not popular at auctions.

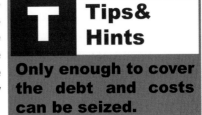

Tips& Hints

Only enough to cover the debt and costs can be seized.

The effect of this is that there may be little of real value in many properties and it will often not be worth the bailiff incurring the expense of actually removing items from the average home.

Quick Questions

Can a bailiff seize a pet?

One question which often arises is whether the bailiff can seize pets? In principle, there is no problem with a bailiff distraining livestock. It used to happen regularly in past centuries and the law is no different now. What has changed is society and the sorts of assets that most people own. That said, if a person has a valuable horse at livery or if they have a pedigree cat or dog, there is no reason why that should not be distrained and sold. If, though, the animal is simply an ordinary mongrel from the dog's home or from cats' protection though, it has no resale value and there is no good reason for listing it.

Bailiffs will seldom seize pets or livestock because of the considerable cost and paperwork involved in transporting them safely, caring for them and arranging sale. An animal will have to be of significant value to make all that extra trouble worthwhile.

No goods or excessive levies
Whatever is seized, the bailiff must also take care to ensure that the quantity seized is not disproportionate to the debt and costs due (the concept of 'excessive levying - for which also see chapter 8). This duty is a long-established principle of English enforcement law and is repeated in the National Standard.

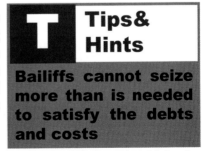

Tips& Hints

Bailiffs cannot seize more than is needed to satisfy the debts and costs

Generally, this duty is understood as meaning that the bailiff should not take far more than is reasonably required to settle the debt. Nonetheless, the reverse situation is also recognised to be just as improper. If there are simply too few

What if there are too few goods to cover the costs let alone pay the debt?

goods to justify a levy - for example, because the sums raised would not even cover the expenses of the process - the bailiff would be acting wrongfully if he continued. Instead he should terminate the levy and return the case to the creditor. This is sometimes called a 'nil goods' or *nulla bona* levy.

There is one defence to the accusation that the bailiff has levied upon an item of too high a value: he may justify his actions by showing that there was nothing else available that he could seize. Of course, the bailiff must be able to demonstrate that he made genuine efforts to find other, lower value goods.

For instance, to justify levying upon a brand new car for a parking penalty of under £100, the bailiff would need to be able to show that he had entered your home and was unable to find any goods of lesser worth - or that he tried many times to enter but was unable to gain access.

The reality is that, for many motoring fines and road traffic penalties, the bailiffs will not try to find other goods. They will be aware of the existence of the motor vehicle and their efforts will be directed entirely to levying upon that. Many of these levies are in danger of being excessive and should be challenged (see chapter 8).

Jointly owned goods

Only those goods belonging to the person in debt may be taken. This includes goods owned both solely and jointly by that person. That said, if jointly owned goods are seized and sold, the proceeds must be divided between the owners according to their shares. This is not always something bailiffs remember to do.

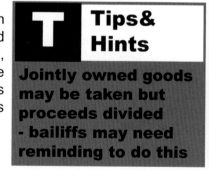

Tips& Hints

Jointly owned goods may be taken but proceeds divided - bailiffs may need reminding to do this

Utility fittings & fixtures

Fixtures that are actually attached (e.g. ranges or cupboards) cannot be taken as they are part of the property, rather than being goods and chattels. The two main factors to be considered when determining whether items are fixtures are the method and degree of their annexation and the object and purpose of that attachment.

On this basis the courts have decided that fitted carpets, curtains and white goods are not fixtures, whilst light fittings, bathroom fittings and fitted kitchen units are. Fixtures are defined as items intended for permanent improvement which could not easily be removed intact.

Finally there are specific exemptions from seizure for pipes, meters and cables belonging to utilities. These are a survival of Victorian legislation, and unlikely to be the subject of problems today.

Goods subject to prior levies

Those items already seized in execution or distress cannot normally be seized again, for instance goods seized in distress for rent cannot be seized in execution. There is an exception to this general rule for the Crown, for which see page 83 above.

Third parties' goods

Assets belonging to lodgers, relatives, strangers and other third parties may not be seized. There are exceptions to this general rule in distress for rent (see page 94 later).

If such items are taken, the person generally has a remedy - such as interpleader (see chapter 8 later) or an action for wrongful interference in the county court (see chapter 8).

A third party may prove ownership by seeking to make in prescribed form a statutory declaration of their position - a sworn confirmation of ownership made before a JP, court officer or solicitor, which could be presented to the bailiff in an effort to avoid the necessity of court proceedings (sample 6, page 100).

Disputes over ownership may arise in connection with strategies taken to defeat seizure as mentioned in chapter 2 or may relate to longstanding claims, particularly those of family members.

Children can purchase, own and dispose of goods in the same manner as adults. Thus, where property is given to a child, it becomes the child's as soon as the gift is made. In consequence items bought by children, or for children, and gifts made to them, should not be seized by bailiffs.

Tips& Hints

Goods owned by children should not be seized.

The National Standard restates this basic legal principle, but adds extra protection by prohibiting bailiffs from seizing items which are "for the exclusive use of a child"- even though (presumably) there might be some legitimate doubt about ownership.

Spouses' and partners' goods

It is not unusual for bailiffs to seek to seize the property of one spouse to satisfy the debts of the other. The existing case law relates to the rights of a married woman, but the general principles will apply to husbands, civil partners and cohabitees as well. See also the earlier paragraph on jointly owned goods.

A married woman may purchase, own, sell and give away any property in all respects as if she is a single person. All property belonging to woman at marriage or acquired by or devolving upon her after that date belongs to her as if she is single. If the items are bought by the husband for the wife's own personal use (e.g. for birthdays, anniversaries or Christmas), they will be gifts. They cannot be seized.

The real problems arise in respect of items bought by the couple after marriage. The courts generally assume an intention to share any property acquired, and divide it up equally. Housekeeping money or property acquired with that will be treated as shared equally unless it is clearly intended to be shared otherwise.

Where there is a joint bank account or other common pool of income, the wages of one spouse are generally seen as being earned on behalf of both. Items bought from such an account therefore would be regarded as jointly owned and seizable. This is not the case where one spouse provides all the income in a joint account, which is simply used as a matter of administrative convenience. The money (and thus the acquisitions) belong to the person providing it.

It is also possible that bailiffs will attempt to levy on goods which are the property of strangers to a household. These items could belong to relatives or friends, having been loaned to you; more likely, they may be owned by commercial organisations - for example:

goods on hire purchase
most probably it will be motor vehicles which will be subject to hire purchase or conditional sale agreements, although furniture and white goods may also be sold in this manner. The essence of hire purchase is that the goods do not belong to the purchaser until the very last payment has been payment. As they remain the property of the finance company, they cannot be levied upon by bailiffs for your personal debts. It will be clear from the agreement what sort of credit has been taken on. The document should be shown to the bailiff.

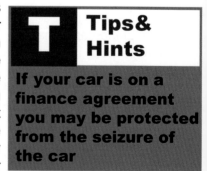

Tips& Hints

If your car is on a finance agreement you may be protected from the seizure of the car

Other finance agreements to purchase cars and furnishings - personal loans from banks and store accounts - are not hire purchase in the strict sense and the items bought will be yours from the outset. The bailiff will therefore legitimately be able to seize them.

leased or hired goods

any items for which a rent are paid are not yours - they remain the property of the finance company. This may cover goods such as televisions and white goods, but the most important are vehicles for disabled persons which are leased from Motability Finance. Regardless of arguments about the propriety of taking a disabled person's car, if the item is leased from Motability, it is theirs and cannot be seized.

Tips& Hints

Motability vehicles which are leased cannot be seized

Tips& Hints

A taxi cannot be seized if it is hired from a private hire company

The same principle applies to cars and taxis hired by drivers from private hire companies. These are both third party property and 'trade vehicles' (see the next section) and, accordingly exempted from seizure.

Readers may sometimes be informed by bailiffs' companies that they are seizing and disposing of a vehicle on HP with the agreement of the finance company involved. The legal justification for this procedure is scant. As should be abundantly clear, the bailiff has no authority to levy upon the vehicle in the first place.

Having done this, any subsequent negotiations between bailiff and finance house should be invalidated by the fact that the bailiff is wrongfully in possession of the goods. In addition, if the hire purchase lender allows the bailiff to dispose of the vehicle when there were no arrears on the agreement or without following the proper procedures laid down in the Consumer Credit Act, the sale could be illegal and could lead to cancellation of the entire credit agreement.

If you are faced with such a situation, complain to the bailiffs, the instructing creditor and to the lender and - if necessary - consider taking the complaint to the Office of Fair Trading.

Statutory exemptions

Basic tools and household items are exempt from seizure in all but VAT and magistrates' court distraint (for both of which see later). The exemptions are:

▶ "such tools, books, vehicles and other items of equipment as are necessary for use personally in business, employment or vocation". This exemption is not limited to tools only capable of being carried by you. However if a tool is occasionally used by another, it is not protected.

Tools will only be protected if they are so essential that without them there is no way that your present business or job could continue. Similarly, motor vehicles will only be treated as a necessity in exceptional cases. Either the vehicle will be needed to continue a job or business or to get to work, or there will be no reasonable alternative; and

▶ "such clothing, bedding, furniture, household equipment and provisions as are necessary for satisfying the basic domestic needs of the person and family". Household necessities are not likely to include stereos, televisions, videos and microwaves.

Quick Questions

What are basic domestic needs, and therefore protected from seizure?

Another approach to the problem of definition has been through codes of practice which often list specific exempt items. The problem with any of these is that they can come to be seen as definitive lists. In fact each case must be decided on its individual facts and merits.

The bailiff will have, at each levy, to exercise discretion in weighing up the interests of you and your household and the creditor for whom they are enforcing and you may of course challenge his decisions and propose your own list of essential exempt items. There is no reason why assets of considerable value might not be protected by the above categories.

In the High Court if a dispute arises as to whether goods fall within the exempt categories, the HCEO may apply for directions from the Court by way of a process called 'interpleader.' The procedure is for you to give written notice of the claim that the goods are exempt within five days of their seizure (the sample interpleader notice given in chapter 8 may be adapted).

The HCEO must then serve notice of this claim on the execution creditor, who has seven days to accept or dispute the exemption. If the creditor does not respond or admits that the items should be exempt, the HCEO withdraws from possession.

If the claim of exemption is disputed, the HCEO seeks directions from the High Court and may also apply for an order protecting himself from any claim for damages. The Court will normally hear and determine the claims summarily. In the county court disputes should be sent in writing to the court and will be referred to a District Judge.

Note that there are three exceptions to these general categories of exempt goods:

business rates
  basic household goods are exempted from seizure in distraint but tools of the trade are not.

the magistrates' court
  the exempt household items are limited to the bedding and clothes used by the person and family. The term bedding should probably be understood to include the bed frame too, but all the same the protection is extremely limited and excludes many basic and essential household items.

  The following 'tools of the trade' are also exempt: "tools, books, vehicles and other equipment that the defendant needs to use in (his or her) employment, business or vocation." It is noticeable that, unlike the general exemption described earlier, there is no requirement that these items are solely used by the individual. In this respect the Criminal Procedure Rules are more generous than other legislation.

VAT distress
  has its own unique list of exempt goods that has recently been introduced. These are any of the following which are located in the home at which distraint is levied and which are reasonably required to meet the domestic needs of any person living there.

  The exempt goods are: beds and bedding; household linen; chairs and settees; tables; food; lights and light fittings; heating appliances; curtains; floor coverings; furniture, equipment and utensils used for cooking, storing and eating food; refrigerators; articles for cleaning, pressing and mending clothes; articles for cleaning the home; furniture used for the storing clothing, bedding or household linen; cleaning articles or utensils for cooking and eating food; articles used for safety in the home; toys for the use of any child in the household and medical aids and equipment.

  On business premises the exempt goods are limited to fire fighting equipment for use on those premises and medical aids and equipment for use there.

  See the table summarising protected goods at page 92.

Table 4: Summary of protected goods

Form of seizure	Basic household goods	Basic tools of the trade	Third parties' goods	Other comments
Execution	standard list see page 90	standard list see page 90	no	jointly owned goods seizable
Local taxes	standard list see page 90	standard list (council tax only) see page 90	no	jointly owned goods not seizable
Fines etc	minimum household items	amended standard list see page 91	no	as above
VAT	expanded list see page 91	very limited see page 91	no	as above
Other statutory distraint	standard list see page 91	standard list see page 90	no	as above
Distress for rent	standard list see page 90	standard list see page 90	in many cases	see details of 'privileges' on pp.94-96

Motor vehicles

Motor vehicles may be seized like any other asset, and are often the most valuable and easily accessible of your possessions. There is almost no legal guidance as to the procedure to be followed when seizing vehicles but it would appear that the same rules of location and entry apply as in any other levy.

Whilst the vehicle itself may be levied upon, there is no reason to suppose that items within it may be taken if that involves forced entry and any such entry is likely to be illegal (see chapter 8).

Tips& Hints

Cars are most likely to be clamped or removed immediately when they are impounded.

Impounding should be by notice, walking possession or removal as already described, but clamping is frequently used. As already described at page 70, the status of this method as a means of placing goods in the custody of the law is very doubtful.

Before removal, a bailiff will normally check ownership with Hire Purchase Information and DVLA. If the results of this are satisfactory, it is normal to remove promptly. When doing this any personal contents in the vehicle are usually either returned to you or listed in the presence of a witness.

Registration documents and keys should be obtained from you or another responsible person (this will enable the car to be sold for a better price). Normally removal is by towing or loading on transporter. Bailiffs should use reasonable care when arranging a contractor to move the vehicle, but, provided this is done, they are not liable generally for any negligence on the part of the contractor. If the car is damaged, owners will have to sue the hauliers, not the bailiffs.

As will have been seen earlier, vehicles are only exempted from seizure if they are essential to a sole trader's business. Vehicles needed for getting to work, for taking children to school or for transporting disabled or elderly family members have no protection in law.

Tips & Hints

If you need a car for work – or are vulnerable – there may be protection from seizure

That said, the terms of the Equality Act and the provisions of the National Standard on the treatment of vulnerable persons, and on the avoidance of discrimination, may provide a basis for arguing that such vehicles should be treated as exempt.

Tips & Hints

If the car's registered keeper is not the owner bailiffs should not seize without correct documentaton

Readers should be alert to the fact that bailiffs frequently blur the difference between the registered keeper of a vehicle and its owner. This not only happens where there is a hire purchase or leasing agreement for the vehicle (see earlier) but where (for instance) another family member may be the actual owner of a car. Very often the problem arises in the context of the enforcement of road traffic penalties.

The regulations relating to penalty charge notices allow the local authority to impose the penalty on the registered keeper of the vehicle; this does not however alter the basic rule that the keeper is not necessarily the owner and bailiffs cannot use the rules on liability to argue that they can seize a vehicle regardless of ownership. Such disputes will need to be settled with documentation. A finance agreement, record of sale or a statutory declaration (see sample 6, page 100) should prove ownership.

The preceding paragraphs have shown that there are a number of potential problems arising from levies on cars. It is a focus of dispute between debtors and bailiffs because motor vehicles are such an attractive item for levying. They are generally accessible, being outside on the drive or street, they can be quickly immobilised without any intervention from you and they are valuable.

A car's worth to the bailiff is not only the better price achieved at auction - it is also the value placed on it by the person in debt and the inconvenience of not being able to use it.

For all these reasons, motor vehicles are a prime target for seizure. This often overrides considerations on the part of the bailiff as to whether it ought to be treated as exempt (for example, a van obviously used for business purposes or a car clearly marked as a private hire minicab) and whether the levy is at risk of being excessive (which will frequently be the case).

In fact, such is the attractiveness of vehicles that it is not uncommon for cars to be seized merely because they are parked outside your home - even though they may belong to a visitor or to a complete stranger!

Conclusions - goods

Always check an inventory carefully, comparing the items listed to the categories described in this section. If you feel that the bailiff has made a mistake, notify the bailiff company. With claims for basic exemptions or goods owned by third parties, they may not be aware there's a problem until you tell them, so act quickly.

The section on page 96 below discusses the consequences of a wrongful levy on goods; chapter 8 looks at your remedies is subject to a wrongful levy.

Levies for rent arrears

Distress for rent needs to be described separately because, in respect of the goods which may be seized, it is the exception to the previous statements:

▶ the basic rule is that any item on the rented premises may be taken, regardless of ownership; but,

▶ this right has been modified by statute and some goods are now exempted, or 'privileged', as the following paragraphs describe.

Readers should note that all the categories of exemption (or privilege) are separate exclusive clauses i.e. tools are protected even if they are not in use.

Tips& Hints

Some goods have protection from levy for rent arrears but not if there are insufficient other goods

Qualified privilege

The items granted 'qualified' or conditional privilege can only be taken if there are insufficient other goods. The landlord may be sued for seizing goods with qualified privilege

Bailiffs - The Law and Your Rights

unless s/he genuinely believed that there were no alternative items. The privileged goods comprise a number of items of little modern relevance but do include tools of the trade in excess of those protected by absolute privilege (see below).

Absolute privilege

Items given absolute privilege are exempted completely from seizure. They include:

Tips & Hints

Items with absolute privilege cannot be touched by bailiffs

perishable items and loose money (i.e. not in a purse or wallet);

the statutory exemptions for tools and household items already described;

goods held in the course of business on trade premises as a direct part of the tenant's business
The trade must be open to anyone and covers all goods taken in during the course of business. This will include items left for repair and goods held by a shopkeeper on sale or return. Conversely, goods purchased by a retailer from a wholesaler will not. Goods held for trade may also have protection from their third party status (see below).

goods on hire purchase or conditional sale subject to a default notice, a suspended delivery order or a termination notice
This is a strange situation where it is actually advantageous to be in debt.

hired and leased goods:
these are not a tenant's property and are exempt from distress.

third parties' goods
The property of lodgers, sub-tenants, strangers and other unconnected third parties is absolutely privileged. If it is seized by mistake these individuals may make a written declaration to the landlord in a set form accompanied by an inventory stating that items levied upon are theirs (see sample 5, page 99).

Such declarations can only be made within a reasonable time after the levy of distress. Sub-tenants must also undertake to pay any rent direct to the landlord until the tenant's arrears are cleared. On receiving a declaration the landlord should return the goods and to continue with the levy would render it illegal. If this is not done the person may apply before two JPs for a restoration order (see chapter 8).

If any such third party goods are sold by the landlord the owner can be reimbursed for their value by the tenant owing the rent.

No privilege

No protection at all is given to the goods of the following:

the tenant's spouse
These goods are the property of a third party, but still can be distrained for rent arrears. However, readers should note that tools of the trade can include items hired or on HP in the spouse's name so that the other spouse can earn a living for the whole family e.g. a sewing machine;

a person who has lent goods to the tenant
Goods on 'permanent loan' with no conditions attached would therefore be seizable; or,

a business partner
although if a person disputes this they can apply to a magistrates' court for the matter to be settled (see chapter 8).

Wrongful levies on goods

As described earlier, a levy may be unlawful as a consequence of the manner of entry or the manner of impounding. A levy may also become illegal as a result of the goods which are seized.

Not infrequently, if the inventory left behind is examined, it will be found that all or most of what has been seized comprises goods which should not have been seized for one reason or another, either because they are exempted or because they do not belong to you.

Bailiffs' companies will sometimes seek to justify this by arguing that they never meant actually to remove any of the items, so no harm has been suffered. This is legally nonsense and is highly disingenuous:

Wrongful levy
it does not really matter whether or not goods are removed from premises: the key stage of the levy process is that of seizure and impounding. It is at this point that the status of your goods is changed by securing the debt against the goods.

Impounding gives the bailiff the right to force re-entry, remove and sell the items listed; it inhibits the owner in how s/he can then deal with the goods. If basic household items are exempted from a levy, it means that they cannot be listed and impounded; it is not acceptable for a bailiff to say "I took possession but I never intended to remove them."

Bailiffs - The Law and Your Rights

Fees

The reasons why bailiffs impound goods they should not impound are not far to seek: the bailiffs are able to charge fees, they are able to insist on payment under threat of loss of the goods and they can report a successful levy to the creditor. Impounding goods which should be

You should not be forced to pay fees for an illegal procedure

exempt is therefore not just wrong as a matter of legal principle - you will be paying for something which should never have been done.

The consequence of a levy on the wrong goods depends on exactly what was listed on the inventory:

Only exempt and non-seizable items listed

The whole levy is wrongful. It is a trespass and will have to be cancelled (along with the associated fees) and started again.

Exempt and seizable items are listed together

In such a case the levy will be invalid in respect of the items which should not have been included on the inventory but will still be valid for those which legitimately could be listed.

However, although the levy may stand, you should note that, having deleted from the inventory the items which should not have been listed, it may be possible to argue that so little is left that the process is not worth continuing - in other words, that the case should be returned to the creditors because there are 'no goods' (see page 85 above).

Conclusions

You should always examine this key stage in the process closely because of the following:

► bailiffs frequently don't (or can't) seize goods correctly;

► bailiffs frequently (try to) seize goods they aren't entitled to; and,

► getting this stage wrong can invalidate the whole process and give access to a range of remedies.

Levy Checklist

Stage	Action	Check
Entry	Household goods seized	Full entry to premises? Where did the 'levy' take place?
Seizure	Inventory prepared	Is there an inventory? Are the goods listed in enough detail? Is there any catch-all phrase at the end? Are enough goods of value listed?
Impounding	Form of impounding used	If a clamp was applied, does the law permit it? If goods were locked up, was this a case of distress for rent? Was the whole shop or factory locked up? Is there a signed walking possession agreement? Who signed the possession agreement? How long ago was it signed? What has happened since? Have any payments been made? Has there been any contact from the bailiff?
Goods	Items claimed by the bailiff What's their value?	Are they your goods (solely or jointly)? Do you know whose goods they are? Are they worthless?
General	Does the bailiff say he's levied?	See what's on the bill Ask for copies of the inventory and possession agreement

Sample 5
Third Party Declaration

To the landlord & bailiff:

1. I the undersigned am the undertenant of [tenant's name] at or {am lodger in or am not a tenant or beneficially interested in any tenancy of or of any part of} the premises known as [address] and occupied by [tenant] {and my undertenancy is not one to which the Law of Distress Amendment Act 1908 is expressed to apply}.

2. The said [tenant's name] has no right of property or beneficial interest in the furniture goods and chattels specified in the annexed inventory and distrained [or threatened to be distrained] by you.

3. The said furniture, goods and chattels are my property [or are in my lawful possession] and are not goods to which the Law of Distress Amendment Act 1908 is expressed not to apply.

* [4. There is no rent due from me to the said [tenant's name] or the sum of £X is due from me to the said [tenant] or future instalments will become due to him on [date] to the amount of £X.

* [5. I hereby undertake to pay you [or the landlord] the said rent so due or to become due to the said [tenant] until the arrears in respect of which the distress was levied [or authorised to be levied] have been paid off.]

Inventory

Date: Signature:

* Only applies to subtenants or lodgers.

Sample 6
Statutory Declaration
(to prove ownership of goods)

I [name] of [address] do solemnly and sincerely declare that:

[in numbered paragraphs explain situation regarding ownership of disputed goods and add list of items claimed to be owned by you].

And I make this solemn declaration conscientiously believing the same to be true, and by virtue of the provisions of the Statutory Declarations Act 1835.

[signature]

[signature of Justice of Peace]

Justice of the Peace for the County of [specify].   * a fee for swearing this will be payable.

Chapter Six
How to Prevent Removal & Sale

Chapter Contents

This chapter will examine:

Payment

As suggested before, the purpose of seizure of goods is to provoke payment through the threat of goods' sale and removal rather than those steps actually being taken.

Removal and sale are costly and awkward and the bailiff would like to avoid them just as much as you would. Consequently the bailiff aims either to either receive a lump sum or to agree instalment payment under the duress of the possible loss of your possessions. Various rules have been developed as to how and when payment can be made.

Instalments

Q Quick Questions

For most people, and especially if you are on low pay or benefi ts, it is preferable to clear any large liability by affordable regular payments. Unfortunately, this is not always easily arranged with bailiffs. It may feel as

Can bailiffs be made to accept instalment payments?

if they are simply being unhelpful, but to be fair the matter is often out of their hands.

Civil court judgments
Bailiffs in the civil courts can be made to accept instalments and withdraw if the court consents to suspending the execution on terms (see page 18). The
terms of such suspensions can be quite low, paid over extended periods.

Magistrates' courts

The court can only postpone a warrant on terms of payment before it is issued. After it has gone to the bailiffs, it is too late (see page 20, chapter 2).

Other types of distraint

In other forms of enforcement there is no option for you to make application to the court and you will have to rely on negotiation with the bailiff or with the creditor.

Contract terms

Difficulties may arise for both you and the bailiff when an affordable payment cannot be agreed. This is often happens because of the time scales for recovery laid down by creditors.

Local authorities will tend to accept instalment arrangements but only for a limited period.

Local authorities may, in respect of local taxes, be happy to see instalments accepted, but will often want them only to run for three or four months. Magistrates' courts and local authorities collecting road traffic penalties do not normally accept instalments at all. In either case if you are on a low income the options open to the bailiff may be limited and removal may be a real threat.

Offering part payment by instalments does not qualify as valid tender of the debt (see below), though of course the bailiff or creditor may accept such a method of settlement and may suspend enforcement until the instalments are completed, rather than withdrawing the levy altogether.

Lump sum payments

In many situations a lump sum payment may be preferable, if not inevitable. There are some legal restrictions as to how payment may be made by the liable person, when it must be accepted by the bailiff or creditor and the impact on enforcement of payment being made.

Reference is often made in the regulations to 'tender' of payment of a debt and costs. It is frequently stipulated that tender should be accepted and this should end the process, the bailiff giving up possession of goods and returning any that have been removed (see page 29, chapter 2 Payment in full).

'Tender' is defined as an unconditional offer to pay the full sum of debt and costs, whether by means of cash, a banker's draft or building society cheque.

The money should be produced at the same time as making the offer. Tender may be to the creditor or bailiff and either should accept.

Offering a current account cheque does not qualify as valid tender, though of course the bailiff or creditor may accept such a method of settling a debt and may suspend enforcement until the cheque is cleared, rather than withdrawing the levy altogether. Refusal of a valid tender also gives you the right to rescue the goods or to issue a claim. For details of the court remedies, see page 140, chapter 8; for details of rescue see page 29, chapter 2.

The timing of the payment which clears the debt has important consequences on what the bailiff can charge and what he is entitled to do next. If tender of the debt and costs is made:

between seizure and impounding
  it would be illegal for the bailiff to proceed to impound or remove.

after impounding
  but before removal, any removal or retention of the seized goods is illegal but does not make any preceding act wrongful.

after removal but before sale
  tender of the debt and costs renders any sale irregular, but not illegal, so that you could only issue a claim for any provable loss.

accruing charges
  despite what has just been said, it is important to appreciate that you do not have an entirely free hand to choose when to make payment. In certain cases, once the bailiff has embarked on a stage in the process, because the costs are accruing by the minute it will not be possible to determine what sum will be required to settle the debt until that stage of the levy has been completed. The

C **Case Study** For example, the High Court decided in the case of *Wilson v South Kesteven District Council* [2000] that, once the bailiffs have actually started physically to remove goods from premises, payment cannot be offered to stop the process until the removal is complete and the bailiff knows what it has cost in terms of men and time.

consequence of payment in full is that, if payment is properly made, the levy will have to be terminated and any impounding agreement will be cancelled. However, special rules apply to bailiffs collecting certain debts:

magistrates' court
It has been decided that bailiffs are not liable on payment of the penalty to return seized goods until they are demanded by you, nor are the bailiffs liable for any damage to the goods. Moreover, some courts refuse to accept payment from the defendant when the warrant is with the bailiff and the bailiff may refuse to take anything but full payment, which can be problematic for you (see negotiations at page 22, chapter 2); and,

Tips& Hints

Be careful with magistrates' courts debts – courts and bailiffs may act inflexibly. Try to find out from each side which is the best payment route to stop the process

Tips& Hints

If you pay for child support or local taxes to stop a sale, you will have to collect goods after payment

child support
maintenance and local taxes
If the sums due are paid or tendered to the creditor or bailiff before sale, the payment should be accepted and the distraint will not proceed. Any sale that has been organised will be cancelled and the goods will be made available for collection by you.

Removal rights

Removal and sale must be viewed by all parties as a last resort where acceptable payments cannot be agreed or maintained. In most cases where goods are to be sold, they will be removed from your premises and stored before disposal at an auction room. Very little is laid down in law as to how this should be done, despite the regularity with which it occurs.

As mentioned earlier in chapter 4, the bailiff may force entry on returning to a property for the purpose of removing goods which were levied upon during a previous visit.

Two conditions attach to this:

Valid prior levy
The right to force re-entry depends upon there having been a full and effective levy on a previous occasion - typically this will have been done

by the bailiff taking walking possession of the goods. If the bailiff merely entered the property, but did not actually carry out a seizure and impounding of goods, he has not progressed beyond the first stage of the recovery process and does not have any right to force his way back in.

However, if there was a valid possession agreement which is still valid and has not been abandoned (see chapter 4), if the agreed payments cease, or negotiations over payment break down, the bailiff will return to remove the goods previously seized in order to sell them.

Forced re-entry

In 1998 in the case of *Khazanchi v Faircharm Investments* the Court of Appeal clarified that force may only be used to re-enter premises if the

bailiff can show that s/he is being deliberately excluded. To demonstrate this s/he will have had to warn you of the planned return so that failure or refusal to permit entry can be interpreted as intentional, thus justifying the use of force. County court bailiffs will also require the permission of a district judge, and even an indemnity from the judgment creditor, before forced entry may be made.

Removal will not usually happen until at least five days after seizure, not including the day of the levy. This timescale is set by statute for some bailiffs, but has merely been adopted as good practice by others.

On removal, only what was previously seized may be taken. If extra goods are discovered after the seizure and notice was presented, they cannot be included in the levy and to remove them would be an illegal second levy (see Chapter 8).

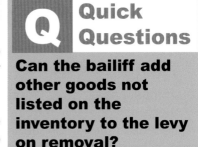

As described in the previous chapter, some firms will try to assert a right to make a 'two stage levy' whereby a catch-all phrase in the inventory purporting to claim "all other distrainable goods" saves them the trouble of conducting a full and thorough search on the first occasion. We saw in the section on inventories that the courts have condemned such lists.

Only the specific items mentioned will have been validly impounded and only those items can later be removed. Any attempt to 'top-up' the levy and add newly found goods will be unlawful.

In distress for rent and execution for road traffic penalties certain procedural requirements apply at this stage.

T Tips& Hints

Watch out for activities that never occurred

Firstly, a detailed breakdown of the costs must be left by handing the person a copy of 'form 9', which is prescribed in the regulations. This details the number of vehicles used, the number of men employed, the number and type of special removal machines, the time spent at the property and loading and unloading the vans and the basic charge for each item. That said, this form can be missed out by the bailiff if all the information is provided in the notice of seizure, form 7.

Secondly, in distress for rent cases, notice of where the goods are stored must be given to the tenant or left at the house within one week of the deposit of those items. If and when removal occurs, the goods should not be removed from the county in which they were seized. The landlord or bailiff may be subject to a penalty if this is wrongfully done.

Care should be taken by bailiffs when removing and storing goods otherwise a claim for negligence could be brought by the owner (see chapter 8). The National Standard requires that a receipt should be left for all goods removed and that they should be handled with reasonable care to avoid damage whilst in the bailiffs' possession.

Bailiffs companies are advised to have insurance in place to cover goods in transit. This should ensure that you are protected and can obtain compensation if an accident should take place.

Public auctions

In most cases, there will be a delay between removal and sale. Sometimes the relevant rules require it (see later). Some delay will be unavoidable because time is needed to organise and advertise a sale; lastly, the bailiffs may be content to allow you a last chance to come up with the money. Until the sale, the bailiff must keep the goods safely and not allow them to be wrongfully used.

The manner of sale varies according to the form of seizure involved, though sale by public auction is normal. In the case of magistrates' court distraint, a person may agree in writing to the bailiff selling by another method. In the county court or High Court either party can apply to court to allow a private sale. In the High Court you can agree to an auction taking place on your own premises if you choose.

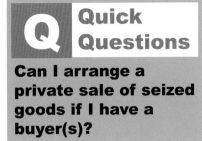

Quick Questions

Can I arrange a private sale of seized goods if I have a buyer(s)?

All the arrangements for the sale are, of course, made by the bailiff and the

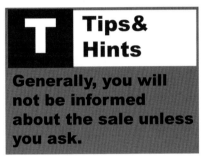

Tips& Hints

Generally, you will not be informed about the sale unless you ask.

person whose goods are being sold will have nothing to do with it. You can still pay off the debt by a lump sum to stop the sale (see page 102) or you could find out when and where the auction is being held and could attend to buy back your own possessions if you wanted (!) - though this makes little sense. Except in county court cases, you will not be informed about the sale unless you ask.

The sums raised by selling second hand goods at auction are rarely going to be high (unless antiques or specialist items are involved). All the same, if you feel matters were mishandled so that the proceeds of the auction were exceptionally low, you can complain on a variety of grounds.

Delay

In many cases there should be a minimum delay of five days before sale (although you can agree to it happening earlier if the goods are perishable, for example). All the same, the sale should be conducted within a reasonable time unless there is good cause. Moreover if the goods are left

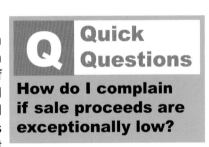

Quick Questions

How do I complain if sale proceeds are exceptionally low?

an unreasonable time on the premises before sale they may have been abandoned, in which case the bailiff will be a trespasser if he tries to collect them (see chapters 4 & 8). Ten days has been held to be reasonable period of time to prepare for a sale.

Best price

The bailiff's duty is to get the best price possible in the circumstances (although it is accepted that auctions will normally be used and that, though low, auction prices represent the best return in the circumstances). There is no requirement to set a reserve price before sale except for income taxes (the Collector will have this done by an auctioneer or some other qualified person). In most cases you can - at your own expense - request that competent persons carry out an appraisement of the goods.

This may not be a worthwhile option, as the expense of having the valuation done may equal or exceed any higher price set by it. This may be compounded by problems selling more costly items through the public auction.

If the goods are of a specialist nature, it is the bailiff's duty to obtain advice on the mode of sale - for instance advertising in specialist press. If goods are sold for substantially less than their value you might be able to bring a claim for damages. However the onus is on you to show that there was substantial difference between the price realised and the real value of the goods at the date of sale.

In the absence of such proof the bailiff will be protected from proceedings. The auction price is not conclusive proof of the value of the goods but it may be very difficult after the event to come up with other proof of the value of your goods.

Mishandling the sale

Failing to get the best price may not be the result of the method of sale chosen; it might also arise from the way the sale was conducted. A claim for damages could be issued if there is evidence of mismanagement of the sale - for example, failing to advertise properly, rushing the auction, attaching unreasonable conditions to the sale or not looking after the goods properly.

Tips & Hints

Failure to advertise properly or other procedural issues may prevent the best price being reached

To summarise, readers should bear in mind that the prices raised at auction are always going to be low. This will mean that, whatever they say, bailiffs are usually very reluctant to remove household goods if it can be avoided. The threat of sale is a means of agreeing payment more than anything but, if it comes to it, the auction will be unlikely to raise enough to clear your debt.

Accounts & the proceeds of sale

The proceeds of any sale should be paid over to the creditor promptly. You are entitled to receive any surplus after the bailiff has paid the debt and costs due and also to recover any goods that remain unsold (though in reality it is extremely unlikely that there will be anything left over). This is often laid down explicitly in the legislation: for example, the regulations for income taxes and VAT require that any surplus shall be returned at the end of the process.

Naturally, creditors will require detailed accounts of the sums collected and charges deducted from them, often on a regular basis. In contrast, there is little regulation on the provision of this information to you. For example:

In the county court
you are entitled, after sale, to a statement of the proceeds raised, the costs charged and the proportion of the debt cleared.

In magistrates' court cases
as soon as is practicable after completing the distraint, the bailiff must send the court a written account of costs and charges. You could then make arrangements to receive this information from the court.

Tips& Hints

In general you will be able to request an account of the sale

In no other form of distress is there such a requirement but it is likely to be done as good practice. For instance, it tends to be done by High Court enforcement officers though there is no duty for them to supply such information. The evidence of such an account may provide the basis for a claim for illegal charges (see chapters 7 & 8).

When can bailiffs try again?

The general rule is that a second distress cannot be conducted. A bailiff can't distrain again for the same debt after a completed levy. To summarise the scenarios covered by this, the bailiff cannot distrain again under a warrant if:

it is for the same debt after a complete levy (there is now no debt due)

if he has levied for too little previously as a result of negligence

Tips& Hints

A second levy is possible under some circumstances

if the bailiff has abandoned validly seized goods (see chapter 4)

if goods levied upon have been wholly lost through negligence on the part of the bailiff

Any further levy would be illegal. If so, the distress may be trespass and you would be entitled to use one of the remedies described in chapter 8.

However, a second levy on the same warrant is permissible where:

there were insufficient goods on a first visit to justify a levy
The bailiffs need not necessarily give up. Instead, they are entitled to wait rather than notify the claimant that there are no seizable goods

the bailiff made a reasonable mistake because of the uncertain value of the items
circumstances at the auction prevented the best price being obtained
For example where demonstrations and threats prevent a sale or a crowd disrupts the auction by harassing bidders and making ridiculous offers

you obstructed or attacked the bailiff or refused entry

the first distress was trespass and thus void (see chapter 8)

the first distress is withdrawn at your request because instalments are agreed
if the arranged payments are not made, the bailiff can distrain again.

T Tips& Hints

Further warrants can be issued

A related issue is the question of when a further warrant may be issued for a debt. Various regulations on statutory distraint permit repeat warrants to be issued, as many times as are necessary, for example, for council tax or child support maintenance. In the civil courts an execution creditor may also issue further or simultaneous warrants.

Conclusions

You should remember that:

► the point of using bailiffs is really to get you to pay, not to sell your goods so don't give up trying to negotiate;

► public auction raises very little, so don't be surprised if a lot is seized and the returns are low (and try to negotiate payment as above to avoid this); and,

► ask for a breakdown of the proceeds (especially to check charges - see next chapter).

Chapter Seven
The Bailiff's Bill

Chapter Contents

Bailiffs' charges are a common area of dispute. This chapter will examine:

What the rules say

The costs chargeable by most bailiffs are regulated by 'scales.' These are tariffs which are found in the various rules and regulations that apply to each form of distress. Typical elements within these are:

► fixed fees for certain activities;

► 'reasonable' costs of removal and storage;

► fees for levies and auctions based on a percentage of the debt; and,

► VAT, which is included in the local tax and child support scale charges, whereas it is additional to charges for distress for rent etc.

In the county court the set charges are much simpler. There is a fee for issue of a warrant. There are then no other charges unless and until a sale occurs.

The point of specifying fees in scales is, of course, to prevent the exploitation of poor and vulnerable debtors. In the past, there were severe problems with bailiffs taking advantage of those in financial difficulties to demand large, extra sums. This problem has still not been entirely eradicated.

Quick Questions

Why are there scales of fees and costs?

The judges have been very clear that no fee should be charged which is not explicitly allowed by the fee scale. This is a fundamental principle of the courts' approach to dealing with fees disputes (see later sections); it is also expressly stated in law for two forms of seizure.

For distress for rent and execution of road traffic penalties, the relevant regulations forbid bailiffs from charging or recovering "any fees, charges or expenses for levying a distress or for doing any act or thing in relation thereto other than those authorised" (rule 10 of the Distress for Rent Rules 1988). In the case of road traffic enforcement, this can be quite a problem (see page 120 later).

Magistrates' court fees

Tips& Hints

For magistrates' court cases, check which region you are in

You should note that in the magistrates' court there is no statutory scale and each bailiffs' firm will negotiate its own fee scale. For enforcement purposes, England and Wales are divided into five regions and the contracts for enforcement work in each are negotiated by HM Court Service.

The bailiff company that obtains the contract will agree its fees with the Court Service. Typically the agreed scales include elements to cover initial administrative costs on the issue of the warrant, attendance and levy charges and charges for removal - particularly of vehicles.

A bailiff can be fined up to £200 for exacting high or improper costs but it is not possible for you to seek detailed assessment (see page118) of charges made during a levy of magistrates' distraint. This is because the procedure only applies where statute sets a scale of charges.

As prosecutions of improper charges are apparently unheard of, this effectively leaves the subject of magistrates' court distress without a remedy for undue charges.

Payment and recovery

As a rule the bailiff's costs are included with the debt due and are recoverable as part of the total sum. Under income tax and local tax legislation it is specifically provided that where payment is made for less than the full sum due (including prescribed costs), it shall be applied to the costs first. It is probably safe to apply this to other regimes unless there is an agreement to the contrary between creditor and bailiff.

In all cases, if the debt is paid, without the costs, before any seizure has occurred the right to distrain ceases. If the debt is paid to the creditor and

the bailiff is instructed to withdraw, the bailiff would not be able to proceed to recover any costs by sale.

This is because the right to fees arises solely from the instruction from the creditor. There is no 'contract' to pay fees between bailiff and debtor. For the same reasons, if the creditor loses the right to enforce, the bailiff cannot sell goods for fees.

Likewise, the costs of previous unsuccessful levies should not be included in later levies as these are only payable out of proceeds of the first and may not be carried over to another: you are under no personal liability for them.

In magistrates' court distraint, costs are **not** added on to the sum if it remains unpaid and the matter returns to the court for further enforcement. This because the penalty due only includes court costs and the court has no liability for any charges, even in cases where the levy is unsuccessful. Only the defaulter can be made to pay.

What bailiffs charge

It is not uncommon for bailiffs to charge for activities not covered by the statutory scales. The activities charged for will include such actions as writing to you prior to levy, setting up and administering instalment payment schemes, taking credit or debit card payments and passing on bank charges to you if a cheque bounces.

It is true that letters and negotiations are specifically allowed for (within limits) in a few scales. For instance, allowance is made for sending a warning latter in road traffic enforcement and for negotiations between landlord and tenant in distress for rent - but other scales do not make allowance for such costs and if they are not on the scale, however reasonable the charges may be, they cannot be recovered.

The reason for the inclusion of these additional charges in the bailiff's bill is clear. The fee scales, although occasionally up-rated, have not been substantially rewritten since Victorian times and the charges allowed are generally low. Most enforcement agencies are now large national companies, with call centres and fleets of vans, and the fee scales were not written with such businesses in mind. Many perfectly legitimate charges are being passed on to debtors.

Sometimes this is done solely at the bailiff's initiative; sometimes it is done with the explicit consent of the creditor employing the bailiff's services. In either case, though, the problem is that these fees are not lawful. If they have not been sanctioned by Parliament, they should not be charged.

The need to generate income from parsimonious fee scales is met in other ways, too. Rather than simply adding on sums which they think they ought to be allowed to charge, bailiffs' companies will take advantage wherever possible of the format of the scale provided by Parliament. This can be done in two ways.

Some of the fees permitted have to be 'reasonable.' It is initially up to the bailiff to set the level of the fee charged, and for the courts subsequently to review this at the request of an aggrieved person, so there are clearly opportunities for raising revenue by setting these fees quite high. Vehicle attendance fees of £150-£250 are a common example of this.

T Tips & Hints

Study your bills carefully

The second means of generating income is to be found in a creative interpretation of the wording of the fee scales and the linked regulations. It is fair to say that the legislation is not always written in the clearest and least ambiguous terms, and this creates further opportunities for income generation by charging the fees earlier than Parliament perhaps intended or in circumstances not anticipated when the regulations were drawn up.

For all these reasons, it will clearly be in the interests of readers experiencing enforcement action to study the bills they have received with some care. Whilst the payment of debts and fees legitimately due should not be avoided, the imposition of unlawful charges is a matter to be investigated.

General fees principles

When considering whether a charge is lawful, certain general principles should be borne in mind. These principles have been devised by the courts over the years and are a useful way of deciding whether a charge is lawful or not. Ask yourself the following questions.

As has already been emphasised, bailiffs may only charge fees which the relevant scale set by Parliament (or the creditor) has endorsed. If fees are made which cannot be

Q Quick Questions

Is it on the fee scale?

matched to the categories allowed by law, they should be queried. They may well be unlawful.

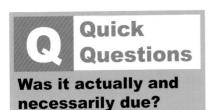

Was it actually and necessarily due?

Just because a fee appears on the fee scale doesn't imply that it can simply be charged. A fee is only permitted if the work has been done to earn it. This entitlement should be evidenced by some sort of document - an inventory or walking possession agreement, for example. The National Standard emphasises this point particularly when it requires that a notice should be delivered to the debtor every time that a fee is charged.

The court must consider if the sums billed are a fair charge for the work done. For example, the court may reduce excessive van charges.

Was it reasonable?

Was it proportional?

Not only will the court consider whether the fee charged is reasonable in itself; it will also want to consider whether it is fair in the context of the debt due. If substantial charges are made for the enforcement of a relatively small debt, especially where nothing has yet been seized, it may be possible to argue that these are disproportionate.

Unlike most of the previous principles, this one is much more a matter of legal interpretation. The court can consider if the charges are being made at the correct stage in the process as envisaged by Parliament; this will involve an analysis of the wording in the fee scale.

Should it have been applied?

What to look for on a bill

The starting point in any dispute will be to gather evidence - you will need to know what you have been charged and what the bailiff was entitled to charge. Readers will therefore have to obtain:

A full breakdown of the bill
This is readily achieved by making a written request for this information under the terms of the National Standard. The bailiffs' company must comply. Make sure all the charges shown on the bill are dated.

A copy of the bailiffs' records
Acquired by means of a Subject Access Request (see chapter 3) could also

be very useful at this point. You could then compare it with the bill you've received and with your recollection of events. You may well discover that you are being charged for activities of which you were unaware.

This does not just mean the odd missed visit, but even a whole levy on goods which has escaped your attention! In such cases, you should naturally demand the supporting paperwork (letters delivered, notices of seizure, inventories and so on). You may even find that the bailiff has seized property you did not even know you owned.

A copy of the applicable fee scale
Ask the bailiff or the creditor to supply a copy of the current scale in operation.

The process of comparing what has been charged, what should be charged and what has actually been done (as evidenced by the documents delivered by the bailiff) may now begin.

If the bailiff states that a levy (or any other action) has taken place but you are unaware of it, ask for the supporting documents. Again, the National Standard requires that the bailiff deliver a notice every time that a charge is made; for some activities, such as levying upon goods, there will have to be some sort of paperwork for it to have any validity at all.

The sorts of potentially challengeable charges to watch out for include the following:

Fees for activities not mentioned on the applicable fee scale
This might include such fees as those for clamping, for damage to or removal of clamps, or taking payment by debit card

Fees for work not done
Especially those which, when queried, turn out just to be a 'warning' or 'indication' of what might fall due if enforcement action continues!

Fees for visits that never took place
There is good evidence that some firms use the initial (and low) visit fees allowed by the scales to cover office expenses such as setting up an account on their IT system and sending a warning letter. The higher attendance fees which are legitimately chargeable later in the levy process are then used to cover the actual first visits to the premises.

Fees not justified by the circumstances
For example, a charge for a van when a car attended or a charge for removal expenses when only walking possession was taken.

Inappropriate use of fees
Charging allowable fees too early in the levy process or charging for activities not contemplated by Parliament. For example, some firms include clamping fees and bank charges under the heading of 'removal expenses'.

Fees that are not justified by the amount of work done
For example, a charge for three levies on three warrants when only one list of goods was made and was carbon copied for all three accounts.

Fees added in pen to notices delivered by bailiffs
The advantage of these is that, if they happen to be challenged, they can easily be denied by the company as an error or over-enthusiasm by the individual bailiff, which could not be done if these were printed on the notices. It seems unlikely, though, that most bailiffs would try to get away with charging amounts not officially sanctioned by their employers.

Fees sanctioned by the client
Some firms will inform you that additional fees have been agreed in the contract with their client (the council or government department to whom money is owed).

This is a mistaken justification. If the fees have been set by Parliament, the amounts cannot be increased nor can extra fees not permitted by the scale be endorsed by a mere local authority or government department. These bodies have no legal power to change legislation and nay such terms in contracts are unlawful and invalid.

That said, it is not unheard of for large bodies such as transport authorities or government agencies to seek to do just this. If such fees are encountered, they should certainly be challenged. In contrast, some local authorities do seek in their codes of practice to limit or cap the fees charged by the bailiffs in certain situations. This is quite legitimate and obviously in your interest.

These are just a few examples of the strategies used to make extra charges over and above the statutory sums. Readers may well encounter others (see also page 120 below).

What you can do to dispute a bill

There are a number of remedies available to individuals aggrieved by the fees they have been asked to pay.

Complain

If you are unhappy with the fees for any reason, take it up with the bailiff company and send a copy to the creditor. If this cannot resolve the matter, consider taking the complaint further to the appropriate trade body or to an ombudsman.

Detailed assessment

Detailed assessment is the process by which a court reviews a legal bill (whether from a solicitor or a bailiff) and approves or reduces the sum charged. Any of the charges laid down in a scale set by Parliament are open to assessment by a county court.

Q Quick Questions

Can I use the court to assess costs?

As already mentioned, the exception from these powers is magistrates' court distraint because the charges are set by the contract between bailiff and the Court Service, and are not laid down in regulations.

Application is made on a 'Part 8 claim form' in the county court within three months of the receipt of the bill (see example application in sample 7, page 124). A hearing is arranged before a district judge at which the bill is examined. Any doubts as to reasonableness should be resolved in favour of the paying party (that is, you). In assessing the reasonableness of charges the court will take into account the following factors:

all the various principles listed in the previous section

the work involved
  If one levy is conducted for several warrants simultaneously, charges may be restricted to those allowable for one levy. The court will take into account the effort involved by the bailiff in preparation, travelling, attendance and follow up reports

the evidence for the basis of the charge
  the court will require the bailiff to substantiate any fee that is charged. It will not only want to see proof of the work having been done; it will also want to know the basis upon which any charge is made. Entirely arbitrary charges unrelated to the actual costs incurred by the company may well be disallowed or reduced.

In assessing fees, the court has two broad powers:

to disallow fees which have not been substantiated or have not been justified as lawful or as having been earned

to reduce fees

This is only possible for those fees which are specified as 'reasonable' and which the bailiff calculates. For example, in council tax levies, if several liability orders are executed at once by the seizure of just one collection of goods, the court may allow only one levy fee under Head B of the fee scale rather than allowing as many fees are there are liability orders. That said, the first and second visit fees under Head A of the scale are flat rate fees which the court has no power to adjust. Provided the judge is satisfied that these visits actually took place, the fees must be allowed in full.

After the hearing the district judge may also make such order for costs as s/he thinks fit, the debt being increased by such costs if awarded against you. Clearly applying for detailed assessment is a risk and could be expensive if it fails.

Beware of costs

Careful advice should be taken first and, unless you can obtain legal help, it may be better to opt for a different remedy. That said, threatening detailed assessment can be effective on its own. Asking for copies of the relevant documents (which will have to be produced by the bailiff company in court in order to substantiate any charge made) may expose the fact that no copies have been retained. Many firms do not keep copies of notices and inventories, blaming the volume of records which would have to be stored, but it puts them in a vulnerable position if any sort of legal challenge is subsequently mounted.

Note also that there is a link between detailed assessment and certification of bailiffs. If during the process of assessment a district judge feels overcharging has occurred of such magnitude that the bailiff's fitness to hold a certificate has been called into question, a copy of the assessed bill endorsed with the judge's opinion is sent to the relevant court and acts like a certification complaint (see also chapter 8).

For and against using the court to assess legal costs

For: the court may substantially reduce bills; link to certification.

Against: complex; can be costly; doesn't apply to magistrates' court distraint.

Pay & claim

An alternative civil remedy for an aggrieved person would be to issue a claim over any charges which were unnecessary or not strictly lawful. In one case, for example, a bailiff distrained for rates on a gold watch and brooch, sold them and retained a sum for costs amounting to six times the debt and reputedly covering removal, storage, possession, delivery to sale yard and haulage. The debtor went to court to recover the excessive fees.

You could start a case like this by issuing a Part 7 claim in the county court to recover the overcharged amount (see sample 8, page 125). See too 'pay and claim' in chapter 8.

Tips & Hints

For and against using the court to reclaim excess charges

For: Simple procedure; relatively cheap; likely to be treated as a small claim by the court.

Against: better suited to illegal rather than excessive charges.

Problem areas

Each fee scale is different and each has its unique areas of uncertainty and dispute. Here we highlight some of the main issues to watch out for when dealing with particular debts. The points made in the section on 'principles' must also be borne in mind.

Road traffic levies

Without doubt the biggest issue with the collection of road traffic penalties is the way they rapidly escalate through the addition of 'removal' fees. Bailiffs companies nationally charge set fees for visits to premises and, at the same time, will add on sums which they decide for 'attendances to remove'. There is no limit to the number of such fees that can be added and, as they are often for £150-200, bills can easily rise alarmingly.

C Case Study The relevant regulations offer some assistance, as the courts pointed out recently in the case of *Culligan v Simkins and Marston Group* **(2009). Every time a fee for removing or attending to remove is charged, the bailiff must issue a breakdown of the amount.**

The judge in the Culligan case felt that the bailiff would be permitted to do without this form where a levy is also conducted as then he should provide prescribed Form 7 (the notice of seizure) which should give a full breakdown of all the fees charged to that point, including any attendance to remove fees.

Many bailiffs' firms neglect to use Form 9, even though Parliament requires that this should be done, whilst their Form 7 notices of seizure are often quite sketchy and do not itemise the fees particularly. In such cases you should argue that any attend to remove fees charged are 'irregular' and should be cancelled from the account.

Council tax

There are two problem areas with the fees charged for the collection of council tax.

The first is for 'attendance fees', which are allowed by Head C of the fee scale. Unlike the fee scale for road traffic penalties, just discussed, the fee scale for council tax spells out the exact circumstances in which a vehicle attendance fee may be charged. The bailiff may make a charge for "one attendance with a vehicle … following a levy."

Tips& Hints

For council tax only one fee for vehicle attendance can be charged

It will be clear from this that this fee can only be charged once and it can only be charged after a levy, which is after a valid seizure and impounding have taken place. Some bailiff firms charge multiple 'attendance' or "enforcement' fees and charge them before they have even got into the premises and found any goods.

The reason for this is simple: the fee is one that the bailiff can set - but this cannot of course justify unlawful practices. Such fees should always be challenged.

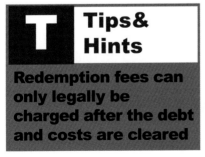

Tips& Hints

Redemption fees can only legally be charged after the debt and costs are cleared

The second problem area is that of so-called 'redemption fees', which are charged under Head H of the fee scale. There has been extensive debate about the interpretation of this fee and what it is supposed to cover. The wording of the regulations is to some extent ambiguous, and this has been used by some firms to justify the charging of this fee very early in the process.

It appears that this fee is meant to cover the bailiffs' wasted costs if goods have been removed for sale but are recovered by you by last minute payment (but this is debatable). What is, however, very clear is that this fee can only be charged when the whole debt has been cleared by the person liable to pay it. Whether this is by lump sum payment or by paying the last of a number of instalments is again a matter of argument, but unless the total council tax debt and the bailiffs' other fees have been cleared, the bailiff is not entitled to make this charge.

High Court enforcement

In the last couple of years, many more individuals have started to face enforcement by HCEOs. They are therefore finding themselves subjected to much higher levels of fees than would have been the case if the county court had enforced the judgment.

Fee charging practices (and levels) vary from firm to firm. That said, there seem to be a number of issues which are common across the country:

Multiple fees
a number firms seem to automatically add to bills all the specific fees allowed by the fee scale (for example, for levying, obtaining a valuation or dealing with interpleader claims). As has been said earlier, fees may only be added to an account if the work to justify has genuinely been undertaken. If you are charged for a

Watch out for multiple fee categories, including things never undertaken

valuation or an inventory or possession agreement, ask to see a copy - you should, in any case, have already received one!

Fee 12
The set fees for mileage and levying are all quite low. Many firms supplement these by using 'Fee 12' on the fee scale. This allows for 'miscellaneous' expenses to be recovered from the judgment debtor.

Watch out for fee 12 - miscellaneous extra charges

It appears from the fee scale that a specific court order may be required before any such charge may be passed on (although very few firms actually do this). What is certain is that some very substantial fees will be added to an account. The problem is any detailed assessment to challenge the charges would have to take place in the High Court, making the process even more difficult for the aggrieved person.

Certainly, readers are advised to examine the bills received from HCEOs very carefully. The issue of a writ of execution will substantially increase the amount payable under the judgment and it is only fair for the person to wish to be satisfied that s/he is being asked to pay what is fairly and genuinely due.

Conclusions

It is regrettably common to need to query charges. Readers should remember that:

► the applicable scale lays down maximum charges but the sum fairly payable may be less;

► extra sums can only be paid by consent, and may not be collected as part of the debt and costs;

► complaints should be brought to the creditor's attention. Extra charges are diverting money from them!

► the remedies available may be good levers to negotiation.

Sample 7
Application for detailed assessment (for council tax)

In the Anyton County Court

Claim number:

In the matter of: the Local Government Finance Act 1992, and the Council Tax (Administration & Enforcement) Regulations 1992.

Between:	A.B.	Applicant
	and	
	C.D.	Respondent

A.B., of XYZ, applies to the court for an order in the following terms:-

1) Detailed assessment under CPR Part 47 of the bill of charges presented by C.D. in connection with a levy of distraint for council tax.

2) Directions as to costs as the court thinks fit.

The grounds on which the applicant claims to be entitled to the order are:-

1) The court has the power to conduct a detailed assessment of charges for distraint under para 3(2) Sch 5 Council Tax (Administration & Enforcement) Regulations 1992.

2) Charges for removal and storage, made under the scale found in para 1 Sch 1 of the above regulations, must be reasonable.

3) Following a levy of distraint on xth x 2011 under a liability order issued by Anyton Magistrates' court to London Borough of X on xth x 2011, the defendants levied upon goods (specify) and submitted a bill showing a charge of £x for removal and storage. A copy of the bill is attached.

4) The applicant submits that these charges are unreasonable in the circumstances.

The names and addresses of the persons upon whom it is intended to serve this application are:-

C.D. Bailiffs

The claimant's address for service is:-

Dated this xth day of x 1997.

Signed:

Claimant

Sample 8
Claim to recover illegal costs

IN THE ANYTON COUNTY COURT
Claim no: 11AD12345

Between:

Mr XYZ   *Claimant*

v

Mayor & Burgesses of the Borough of XX   *1st defendants*

And

ZZ Bailiffs   *2nd defendants*

Statement of claim

Give details of events in numbered paragraphs-

1)
2)
3)

Setting out the background- who instructed the bailiffs, who they are and what they were collecting. Explain what was paid to them under protest and what charges are disputed as unlawful (and why).

4)
5)
6)

AND the claimant claims:

1) REPAYMENT of the sum of £XXX;

2) INTEREST thereon; and

3) COURT FEES.

Dated this   day of   2012.

Signed:

The Bailiff's Bill
125

Fees Checklist

Check	Action
Have you got the key information- bill/ fee scale etc?	No? ask for copies
Do the figures given to you by bailiff add up?	No? Then query the bill
Do the figures given to you by bailiff match the figures on the official bill?	No? Then query the bill
Can you match the fees charged to the fee scale?	No? Then ask for clarification
Can you match the fees charged to the paperwork you have received?	No? Ask for copies of any missing document; seek clarification
Can you match the fees charged to your version of events?	No? Then query the bill
Is the fee charged necessary and justifiable?	No? Then query the basis of the charges
Is the fee charged reasonable for the work done?	No? Then query the item
Is the fee charged reasonable compared to the original debt?	No? Then challenge the bill as disproportionate

Bailiffs - The Law and Your Rights

Chapter Eight
What to Do if Things Go Wrong

Chapter Contents

This chapter will examine:

Complain to the bailiffs

If you have any concerns or grievances, these should always be taken up first with the bailiff company which called on you. You will have the name and mobile phone number for the bailiff who called as well as the address of the company. Unless you are simply trying to arrange to make a payment, there is seldom much to be gained raising a complaint with the bailiff.

Most companies of any size will have some sort of complaints department or customer care team: always take matters up with them directly and always do this in writing so that you have a record of what was said and you can be sure to set it all out clearly and fully. If the problem cannot be resolved this way, you can next try the creditor or the bailiffs' professional body (see pages 129 and 164 for more on these).

Complain to the creditor

Any problem should obviously be taken up initially with the bailiff's firm. If this is not successful you may turn to the creditor instructing them. One should also keep that organisation informed of any earlier negotiations by copying all correspondence to the relevant officer or department.

In most cases there will be a written contract or service level agreement between creditor and bailiff, the purpose of which is to regulate the general administration of enforcement by distress and to ensure that recovery is conducted in an acceptable manner.

Two aspects arising from the contractual relationship need to be considered:

Agency

Regardless of the detailed terms of the contract, the effect of it will be to make the bailiff the 'agent' of the creditor. The meaning of this is that the bailiff, as agent, has the authority of the principal (for instance, the local authority) to act on their behalf as an intermediary with third parties (i.e. you). In this the agent has the powers of the principal, but cannot exceed those powers.

Thus, where statute gives a local authority the power to levy distraint in a certain way, the bailiff may exercise those same powers, but may not go beyond them. There is an implied authority to do all subordinate acts necessary or incidental to the exercise of these powers (though these may be restricted by codes of practice and the like - see page 37, chapter 3).

Generally the principal will be responsible for those acts of the agent that are expressly authorised or are within the scope of the agent's apparent or implied authority. Thus the principal may become responsible for acts of illegal seizure and may be taken to court along with or instead of the bailiff (see later in this chapter).

If the act in question is completely outside the agent's authority, however, there can be no joint liability. For example in a case in 1885 a water company was not held liable for an assault committed by a bailiff executing a warrant in their name as such an excessive action was not within the fair scope of the bailiff's duty.

Tips & Hints

You can use some creditors as a moderating influence, and you have little to lose by trying

The value of this legal relationship of the creditor and bailiff to you is that there is a third party who can be involved in any dispute with the bailiff and who, besides being another defendant to be sued if court action is taken, may act more impartially as a moderating and supervising influence in negotiations.

Quick Questions

For and against complaining to the creditor?

For: Cheapness; accessibility; speed; effectiveness because of the desire to avoid 'bad publicity'.

For: If a complaint is upheld, the creditor can refer it to the county court certificating the bailiff for the matter to be treated as a certification complaint.

Against: Unwillingness of creditors to intervene; low or nil compensation.

Complain to professional associations

The professional and trade associations representing bailiffs have disciplinary codes and complaints procedures for members that may be turned to for arbitration if attempts to negotiate fail, or as an alternative to them.

High Court Enforcement Officers Association
exists to regulate its members, maintain professional standards and to lobby government. It has a code of practice and a disciplinary procedure for dealing with complaints against members. See their website for details – see page 164.

Civil Enforcement Association
represents many of the private bailiffs' companies and individual certificated bailiffs. It too has a code of practice and a disciplinary procedure for dealing with complaints against members. See their website for details – see page 164.

The strength of all these voluntary codes depends on how well they are used. This in turn depends on the firms publicising the procedure, which can be a problem. Also these procedures only tend to apply if internal complaints processes have been exhausted. Again, whether these will be invoked depends on how information is passed onto people by bailiffs. Aggrieved individuals should always seek a clear, full statement of how their problem will be handled.

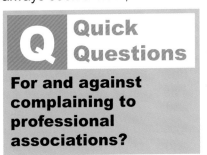

Q Quick Questions

For and against complaining to professional associations?

For: Cheap; quick; accessible.

Against: Concerns about impartiality; largely untested; low levels of compensation.

Complaints to Ombudsmen

This remedy may be used where there has been maladministration by a local or central government department which has involved the use of bailiff's services. The aggrieved person may complain to the relevant ombudsman - for example, the Local Government Ombudsman for local authorities or the Revenue Adjudicator for the Inland Revenue and H M Customs.

The sort of maladministration that could form the basis of the complaint includes such issues as error, illegal acts and failure to act (that is, neglect and delay), failure to follow proper procedures or giving misleading (or inadequate) information (see also chapter 3).

If a complaint is upheld following investigation by the ombudsman it is usual for them to recommend review of and improvements in administration and the award of compensation to the individual. Bailiff related problems fairly frequently form the basis of complaints to the Local Government Ombudsman, typically arising from poor communications between the council and bailiffs and failure to keep adequate records and accounts.

Quick Questions

For and against complaining to the Ombudsman?

For: Cheap; accessible; may be compensation; creditor may be told to improve procedures.

Against: Slow; may just get an apology.

Court action for wrongful levies

It is always preferable to resolve a complaint informally. It will be easier, quicker and less expensive. However, if this route fails, a person may always resort to court action, or at least the threat of it.

There is a range of remedies available for use in cases of wrongful actions by bailiffs. Whether these are accessible, either because of the cost or the complexity of court procedure, is another matter.

Nonetheless, sounding sufficiently well informed and confident may be a lever to (re)start negotiations with a creditor or bailiff. Dealing with complaints absorbs staff resources and money. It is surprising how often cases are returned to creditors, or are settled as a good will gesture, as soon as questions are asked.

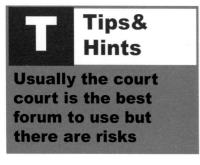

Tips& Hints

Usually the court court is the best forum to use but there are risks

The following sections assume that readers will take county court action themselves, and describe the procedures on this basis. It may be necessary to do without legal assistance either because the dispute is over a relatively small amount, for which legal aid is not available, or because your income disqualifies you from getting legal aid. In such cases, the best course of action may be to issue a county court claim for compensation under £5000. There are two main reasons for advising this:

Court fees
> the lower the claim, the lower the court fee - though you may be entitled to have the fee waived or remitted because of your income

if the bailiff decides to fight the claim, and it is for less than £5000, it will be classified by the court as a 'small claim.' This means brings several advantages to you as the claimant:

Costs - even if you ultimately lose the case, you are very unlikely to have to pay any of the other side's legal costs;

Process - small claims are much simpler and quicker to get ready for hearing. There are no large amounts of complex documentation and hearings usually take place within 6 months. The courts can provide all the necessary forms to you as well as guidance leaflets on how to complete and issue them;

Hearing - the case will be heard relatively informally in private at the court, sitting around a table in a district judge's office.

For all these reasons, although firms may initially (threaten to) defend a small claim, the matter is often settled before the hearing for purely commercial reasons: it is cheaper for companies to do so than to incur the time and expense of attending court. In addition, given the uncertainty over some aspects of bailiff law, it may be more prudent for a company not to risk an adverse decision by the court.

Tips& Hints

Take legal advice if your claim is worth more than £5000

If you genuinely believe that your damages claim against a bailiff company exceeds £5000, you are strongly advised to seek legal advice, both on the value of your claim and on the strength of your case. Any defended claim for a larger amount may be sent for trial in open court. This is a much longer and more costly procedure and, if you are unsuccessful, you will have to expect to pay the other side's legal bill - which could be substantial.

Although for a claim in trespass you can leave the assessment of damages to the discretion of the court, it is not necessarily a good idea simply to claim a sum "...Not exceeding £5000" (£5000 being the present upper small claims limit).

There are two reasons for this. First of all if you claim a figure not exceeding £5000 then your claim fee will be the fee which is applicable for a £5000 claim and this can be a figure approaching £300. If instead you ask the court to award you a sum "... Not exceeding £1500" then you will only be charged the fee for a £1500 claim.

This second reason for reducing the value of your claim is to keep it modest. You should try to make a realistic assessment of what you feel you have lost as a result of the bailiffs trespass in terms of humiliation or the assault upon your rights.

A court is very much more likely to appreciate a claim which appears to be levelheaded and moderate. If you are able to justify the sum that you are claiming by means of a clear and logical explanation, then the court is more likely to access your claim and to award you what you are asking for.

Do not start trying to claim the maximum possible figure simply because you are angry or you are outraged. Try to take a rational view and you will stand a greater chance of success.

Court action can be taken to find a remedy for any "wrongful" act by a bailiff. This could take one of three forms - illegal, irregular or excessive. You should note that attempts to levy can be as wrongful as actual levies, and the same remedies will apply.

Illegal levy

An illegality is any act that is forbidden by law. A bailiff would be acting illegally if:

there is no right to distrain (e.g. the debt has been paid, or its amount tendered);

if the wrong address has been visited; or,

if an unlawful or unauthorised act is committed during the levy, such as seizure of exempt or third party goods or following a forcible entry.

The effect of showing illegality is to make the distress into trespass and void from the beginning. Thus, proving a levy to have been illegal can both recover the goods seized and/or damages and also terminate the levy completely (though the bailiff could try again.

Note that illegal execution is trespass but the levy remains good. To put it another way, illegal execution does not necessarily affect the validity of subsequent seizure or sale, unlike the illegal distress described above, but the person can still issue a court claim.

The execution is not automatically void. However, an execution is void and is trespass from the start if the debt was paid.

Irregular levy

An irregularity is anything done in the wrong manner or without the proper formalities. A court may award damages for any losses caused by it but the validity of the act done is not affected - in other words, the levy is not void as with an illegal act. An irregularity occurs when the levy is correct but subsequent events are not - for instance, sale of goods at an undervalue or a failure to give proper notices.

Irregularity is more of a technical offence than illegal distress and, as the remedy is only compensation for the actual damages suffered by the claimant (which may be negligible or difficult to prove depending on the nature of the irregularity). As a result, it is often not worth pursuing.

You should note that the distinction between illegal and irregular distress is something created by Act of Parliament. In other words, wrongful actions by the bailiff are only converted to the less serious offence of irregular distress if an Act says this is to happen.

Irregular distress applies to the following forms of seizure of goods:

- for rent arrears;
- for council tax and business rates;
- for county court judgments;
- for road traffic penalties;
- for magistrates court fines etc; and,
- for child support maintenance.

This means that technical errors in levying distraint for income taxes, VAT and the like and in levying execution in the High Court may render the entire process a trespass and void from the start.

Excessive levy

This occurs when more goods are taken than are reasonably required to satisfy the debt and costs. Judging the value of the goods must take into account the nature of the sale which will have to take place: as described in chapter 6, an auction sale of seized goods is never going to raise an especially good price. Furthermore, there will be no basis for a claim if there was only one thing to take, even if its value greatly exceeded the sum due.

Because they often fail to appreciate the nature of sale at auction and the prices likely to be raised by the process (plus the natural tendency to overvalue one's own goods) people often feel that there has been an excessive levy when there has not. Indeed, the courts have warned that debtors should expect a generally sceptical reaction to their own estimation of the goods' worth. Consequently, it is fair to assume that successful actions for excessive distress will be rare.

Note: it is wrongful for a bailiff to levy excessively; it is also a breach of the National Standard which prohibits disproportionate seizures. See too the discussion of the subject at page 85.

Issuing a claim for damages for an illegal levy

Where an illegality has occurred either you or the owner of any goods seized could issue a court claim to recover some compensation. Generally this would be either a claim for trespass to land or trespass to goods. It is also possible to issue a claim for trespass to person (i.e. assault and/ or battery) but it may be difficult to prove and is far less likely to arise.

Claims for trespass are all made on the same county court form (the Part 7 claim form). The difference will partly be the facts described, but more importantly will be the remedy requested. In claims in respect of trespass to goods, it may be possible to ask for an order for the return of the goods.

Trespass to land

Every unlawful entry into or on to premises is a trespass for which court action may be taken, even though no actual damage is done. Thus it is trespass for a bailiff to levy in an illegal way or to remain on the property after a legal seizure has become illegal. The fact that the bailiff either had no right to enter or abused a legal right of entry gives the claimant an automatic right to damages.

The case is begun by applying for issue of a county court Part 7 claim form (form N1) seeking damages. Claims may be made against the bailiff who levied and/or any creditor authorising the illegal act as the bailiff's principal.

The claim form itself has space for the claim (if reasonably short and concise) to be described on the rear of the form. If more detail is required, a separate 'statement of claim' should be prepared on a separate sheet of A4 (see example at page 153, Sample 9).

The bailiff will receive the claim form with a 'response pack' enabling him to either admit the trespass or to defend the claim. If it is defended, the case will go to trial at court. How the matter will be heard will depend on the level of damages you have claimed.

If you have capped your claim at £5000 the matter will most likely be dealt with as a 'small claim' and will be heard by the more informal process of arbitration. The major advantage of this is that if you are unsuccessful, you will not have to meet the defendant's legal costs, though some witness expenses may be payable.

If the sum claimed is over £5000, but under £25000, the case will be tried before district judge. If the sum exceeds £25000, trial will be before Circuit Judge. In either case the procedure is more formal and the losing party may expect to pay the other side's legal costs (barrister, solicitors etc.) as well as their own.

Even if the claim is not defended, and the claimant wins by default, there will still have to be a hearing as the judge will have to hear the details of the case in order to assess the damages that are awarded. These do not have to be substantial - a token sum could be awarded in acknowledgment of the fact that a trespass occurred, although it was not serious. As we have seen, it is best to make a moderate claim to give yourself the best chance.

However if specific losses can be shown an additional award of special damages may be made to compensate for this. Special damages may cover repairs to detached fixtures or other damage to property; the full value of exempt goods seized and sold; injury to the reputation of business premises; or sums paid to release goods (see also 'pay and claim' later).

Wrongful interference with goods
This covers a number of wrongful acts by a bailiff:

illegal seizure and removal
the taking of goods s/he was not entitled to levy upon, either because they were exempt or belonged to someone else

damage to goods during removal or storage through mishandling or negligence

disposing of goods the bailiff was not entitled to sell

detaining goods depriving the owner of the use of them whilst they are impounded

T Tips& Hints

Use form N1 to claim for wrongful interence with goods

The court claim should be issued in the county court on the Part 7 claim form by the person who owns the goods - or who had them in their keeping at the time. On the claim form you could ask for:

damages
(best capped at £5000) for loss of goods, for damage to them or for loss of use of them;

an injunction to stop sale
(if necessary)

an order for the return of the goods if the bailiff is still holding them
These orders are only rarely made except for specific, irreplaceable items. Usually the court will feel that monetary compensation is an adequate remedy. Even if an order is made, the goods are only likely to be recovered at the end of lengthy court proceedings.

If you believe you are entitled to damages exceeding £5000 or you are determined to try to recover the specific goods taken, it will be best to seek legal advice and to possibly try to obtain legal aid.

For and against seeking damages for an illegal levy?

For: Relatively accessible and inexpensive; probable award of damages.

Against: Quite slow to get a decision; will be court fees to pay up front (though those on means tested benefit are entitled to fee exemption and others can claim remission on the grounds of hardship) and possibly expenses to other side if lose; unfamiliar jargon and procedures; damages may be low.

Against: The procedure is unlikely to recover specific consumer goods, as an award of damages will be considered to be adequate compensation.

Injunctions

Injunctions are court orders instructing a person to refrain from doing certain acts (e.g. forcing entry, removing or selling goods).

They are available in the county court as an adjunct to a damages claim - in other words, the court cannot grant an injunction alone - there must be at least the basis of a case to sue the bailiff for damages.

You can seek an injunction – but only with a damages claim

There are a couple of attractions to applying for an injunction:

1. a county court can make one as a matter of urgency if needs be. It is possible for a person to attend court and make the whole application within a matter of hours; and,

2. although the theory is that an injunction cannot exist without a claim, many courts will not insist that a claim is actually issued once the injunction is made. It is sufficient to have a draft claim form on the court file. That said, in many cases, readers will feel aggrieved enough to want to pursue a claim for compensation.

Application is made by completing form N16A stating the terms of the injunction sought - for instance to prevent forced entry to premises and removal of goods.

Tips & Hints

Use form N16A to seek an injunction, form N285 for the affidavit, N1 for the damages claim

In support of this an affidavit must be sworn on court form N285 giving the grounds for the application - for instance, describing the bailiffs' illegal acts and what further action is threatened.

These will be supported by a Part 7 claim form setting out the facts of the case and making a claim for damages and for an injunction against the bailiffs. As stated, it is up to you whether or not to pay the extra fees actually to issue this as well as the injunction.

The application is made 'ex parte' with only you present at the court. If the district judge is satisfied that matters are urgent and justify it an injunction could be issued immediately to the bailiffs. Whether or not the court has already made an injunction in an urgent case, there will be a hearing a few days later, typically before Circuit Judge, to decide whether to confirm the terms of the order for a longer period. An injunction is issued by the court on form N16 and the bailiff can be committed for breaching it.

The courts will take account of several factors in injunction applications:

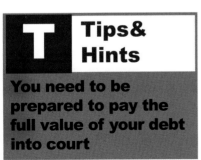

Tips & Hints

You need to be prepared to pay the full value of your debt into court

the parties' legal rights
the courts do not favour interfering with the legal right to distrain, so there must be both a serious error by the bailiff plus an imminent threat of loss of essential goods, or assault or damage to property, to persuade the court to intervene.

payment into court
the court will not normally make an injunction unless it is satisfied that any person prevented

from enforcing a legal claim will be in the same position, in the event that their claim turns out to be right, as if the court had not interfered.

The court usually achieves this by making an injunction conditional on the claimant paying all the debt into court, upon which the bailiff is ordered to withdraw. Thus the utility of the injunction is tempered by its possible expense to the claimant.

Quick Questions

For and against seeking damages for an illegal levy?

For: Speed; effectiveness if granted; sanctions for breach.

Against: Cost; may only grant in rare cases; fairly complex procedure.

Damages for irregular distress
You can issue the claim on the Part 7 claim form. Creditors can be included in the claim if they authorised the distress, though not the irregular act, as their duty is to ensure proper enforcement.

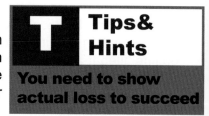

Tips& Hints

You need to show actual loss to succeed

The problem with these claims is that you can only recover what 'special damages' can be proved. These are based on the actual losses suffered.

In the absence of proof of special damages, the claimant cannot even get a nominal sum of compensation. Special damages need to be proved if, for instance, the bailiff sells within five days, sells without appraising or sells without serving the proper notice. For these reasons, it may seldom be worthwhile actually issuing such a claim.

Damages for excessive distress
The claim will be conducted as for irregular distress above. The excess will have to be shown to be substantial rather than trifling. The price realised at sale is the best evidence of the items' value and will be the basis upon which damages are assessed.

Tips& Hints

Use form N1 to start the claim even if the goods are not yet sold

A claim can be begun on Part 7 claim form (N1) - even when the goods are not yet sold - the amount of damages claimed then being the loss and inconvenience occasioned by the goods' removal. If there is no inconvenience, as in walking possession, no damages may be awarded.

Bailiffs - The Law and Your Rights

For: Relatively accessible and inexpensive; possible award of damages.

Against: Quite slow to get a decision; will be court fees and possibly expenses to other side if lose; unfamiliar jargon and procedures; damages may be hard to prove.

Replevin

Replevin is a remedy to obtain recovery of goods that have been illegally seized. It is used rarely because of its obscurity and cost.

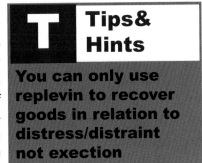

Tips& Hints

You can only use replevin to recover goods in relation to distress/distraint not exection

Replevin applies to statutory distraint as well as to distress for rent. It is not applicable to execution in the High Court. Seizure under the order of a county court or magistrates' court cannot normally be replevied unless the warrant in question was issued in excess of or completely outside the court's jurisdiction - both of which will naturally be unlikely, although enforcing an invalid order or one that had been cancelled might be examples.

Replevin only applies in cases of illegal conduct. It could therefore be used, for instance, where there was no debt due, where an illegal entry occurred or where exempt goods were seized.

The use of replevin bars other remedies and is an alternative to a claim for wrongful interference with goods. However, the bailiff may still be sued for trespass to land (say, for forcible entry), even after a replevy, as the remedy relates to wrongful interference with goods alone and does not provide any compensation for any trespass to the premises themselves.

The claim may be brought against the bailiff, the authorising person, or both. It is begun in the county court, the powers being found under s144 and Sch.1 County Courts Act 1984. Replevin consists of two parts.

Tips& Hints

There are no standard forms to start replevin claims

the replevy
The owner of the goods presents a notice in the county court (see Sample 10 - there are no standard forms) stating the facts. At the same time you will have to provide a replevin bond (security) and give an undertaking that a court claim will be commenced within four weeks.

The district judge then instructs the court bailiff to return the goods to you. The level of security required is set by the district judge at a figure considered sufficient to cover the probable costs of the case and the alleged debt. The security could be a solicitor's or bank's undertaking to pay or a bond by sureties.

You must then begin the action without delay and undertake to return the goods if ordered. Note the need for security in replevin is one of its major disadvantages. Often security from a third party is unavailable and the only option will be paying the disputed debt into court, which may be similarly impossible.

the action

You will then have to issue a claim for an illegal levy, in order to prove that the bailiff wrongfully took your goods and that you were entitled to get them back.

Tips& Hints

See sample 11, page 154 for an example claim

A hearing follows with the bailiff as defendant. It will be necessary for you to show that the levy was illegal. If successful, the owner recovers the expenses of the replevy plus damages which are assessed as the value of the replevin bond itself plus any actual damages suffered by reason of the illegal levy.

These could be compensation for loss of the goods and for annoyance and injury to your reputation. No further claim could then be made for compensation in respect of the goods. If the bailiff is successful in defending the claim, s/he is entitled to an order for the return of the goods and the security is forfeit. Costs may be awarded at the discretion of the court.

Replevin is attractive as it offers immediate recovery of goods, contrasted to a potential wait of many months in a case for wrongful interference. Moreover, return of the goods is guaranteed in replevin, whereas it is rare in wrongful interference cases.

However, it is a little used and little known remedy. Procedurally, it is not straightforward: there are no standard forms to use and you face paying the other side's legal costs if you lose. You may need to think carefully and take legal advice before you embark on this course of action; a claim for damages may be preferable.

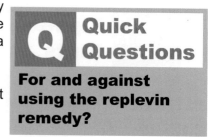

Quick Questions

For and against using the replevin remedy?

For: Can recover goods quickly; may get award of damages.

Against: Obscure; possibly expensive because of security and because of the risk of legal costs as the case is not treated as a small claim; limited coverage of forms of distress.

"Pay & claim"

A fairly simple remedy could be to pay the debt subject to dispute and then make a county court claim to recover some or all of the sums paid on the grounds that they were wrongfully demanded and were paid under duress. Such an claim is not a claim for damages: all that can be recovered is the sum paid, but with no added compensation (see page 125, Sample 8 earlier).

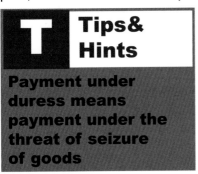

Tips& Hints

Payment under duress means payment under the threat of seizure of goods

Duress in the context of a bailiff's levy means the compulsion under which a person pays money to the bailiff through fear of their property (or the property of a close family or household member) being wrongfully seized or detained.

The levy in question may be threatened or actual. The payment must not be made voluntarily - it should made under protest. This should be made clear in words or in writing at the time of payment, ideally, but the court may find that the circumstances of payment or your conduct are enough indication of your intention.

Establishing that payment was made under protest is important because the general rule is that lawful seizure by a bailiff is not duress or illegal pressure and, as a result, any payment made by the person to release their goods is simply submission to the lawful enforcement of a debt.

Consequently, there must be some wrongful element in the levy and you, in paying, would have to make clear that payment was not seen as an end to the matter but simply a way of retaining use of the goods rather than being deprived of them during lengthy litigation over the alleged illegality.

Tips& Hints

This remedy is ideally suited for clamping cases, where getting the goods back quickly is the key. Use form N1

This remedy is particularly well adapted to cases where the fees charged are disputed or where the goods seized were urgently needed - for example, payment was made to release a vehicle from a clamp, although the right to clamp was not itself admitted.

This remedy is commenced issuing a Part 7 claim in the county court. This should be filled in setting out the facts of the incident, explaining what was considered to have been done illegally and why and demanding repayment of the sum paid, plus interest and court fees. If successful, the claim will lead to a judgment for repayment of the sums demanded. These cases are often settled by bailiffs' companies long before they get to court.

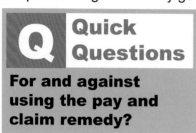

For and against using the pay and claim remedy?

For: Very simple; fairly quick

Against: Court costs may be payable; only get back sums paid, not damages or goods

Certification

A bailiff must hold a county court certificate in order to levy for rent, local taxes and road traffic penalties. In addition, most other creditors will prefer to use certificated bailiffs even though this is not mandatory for them to do so.

The certificate authorises the holder to levy anywhere in England and Wales during a period of two years. A bailiff may be fined for levying without a certificate; such a levy would also be a trespass.

Certification offers individuals in debt two benefits:

1. some guarantee of the knowledge and suitability of the individual bailiff;

2. the ability to complain about the bailiff through the county court if something goes wrong.

The procedure for granting and revoking certificates is found in the Distress for Rent Rules 1988. The 'issuing' county court can grant a certificate only if it feels that the applicant is a fit and proper person and has an adequate knowledge of the law.

It is fair to say at present that the certification process is not much of a test of an applicant's suitability or knowledge. Each court must compile and display a list of all bailiffs holding certificates issued there on February 1st each year.

Where can I find out if a bailiff is certificated?

More usefully, a central register held by the Court Service (which can be consulted online – see page 164 for web address) or, alternatively, you may ring Court Service on 0203 334 6355.

If a complaint is planned, it will be important to check the details of the bailiff to discover whether s/he holds certificate and from which court. If the individual who called was not certificated, it should still be possible to make a complaint against the employer if s/he is certificated, on the basis that unqualified staff were used for work for which a county court certificate was mandatory.

Tips & Hints

If uncertificated staff are used, you may have cause for complaint. Use form 4 to do so.

It should also be possible to use the certification process to complain about the actions of certificated bailiffs even when levying for debts for which no certificate is required. The basis for this is that, as has been seen, many of the principles of bailiff law are common across the board. If a bailiff makes a serious error collecting, say, a fine, it can be argued that this indicates a general unfitness and lack of knowledge.

Any complaint as to the conduct or fitness of a bailiff should be made to the court which issued the certificate. A standard complaint form (Form 4) is available from county courts or online (see page 164 for web address).

The court must then send written details to the bailiff who must reply in writing within fourteen days, or a longer period if the court allows. A hearing should be arranged before a Circuit Judge to explain why the certificate should not be cancelled if the bailiff either does not reply or the reply does not satisfy the Judge that the person remains fit to hold a certificate.

The bailiff is ordered to attend and the complainant and any other interested party receives a copy of the reply. At the hearing the bailiff should attend and make representations, as may the complainant . The procedure at the hearing is determined by the Judge, including what evidence shall be allowed, and the hearing may proceed even in the bailiff's absence.

After hearing the parties, if the complaint is upheld the Judge may cancel the certificate and/or may order that the security be forfeited either wholly or partly to compensate the complainant, to cover any costs and expenses s/he may have incurred and also to cover the court's own costs, expenses and fees.

Quick Questions

What will I get if I win my complaint?

The court publicises the cancellation both locally and nationally if the bailiff operates outside the district of that county court.

Tips& Hints

Specifically request that the levy is prevented from continuing

It should be noted that even if a certificate should be cancelled, it continues to have effect for any possession agreement entered into before the date of cancellation unless the Judge directs otherwise. It will be necessary for a person to make a specific request for an order from the court to prevent any levy continuing.

The attractions of this procedure to the complainant are its simplicity and its cheapness, as no filing fees are incurred.

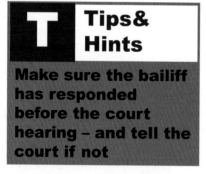

Quick Questions

What are the risks of this course of action?

The attitude of courts is likely to be that the wrong complained of will have to be very serious, and certainly more than a 'technicality', to warrant revocation or a heavy financial penalty.

Readers must heed a significant warning about 'form 4' complaints against bailiffs. It appears that this remedy may have been overused - and used in inappropriate cases - in recent years and bailiffs have responded by trying to recover their legal costs in cases in which the complainant fails.

This has been facilitated by courts, which do not always follow the procedure laid down in the 1988 Rules. Complaints are increasingly treated by courts as normal cases going to trial in front of a circuit judge. Because of this, the losing party will normally be found liable for the other side's legal costs, and these can easily run into thousands of pounds.

Tips& Hints

Make sure the bailiff has responded before the court hearing – and tell the court if not

For this reason, the advice only to use this procedure in cases of grave abuse by a bailiff must be re-iterated.

Secondly, readers are strongly advised to examine the papers received from the court - if a hearing is immediately arranged before the bailiff has even responded to the complaint, you will need to contact the court office to point out that this is not what the Distress for Rent Rules 1988 say. If needs be, you may have to complain to the Court Manager.

For: Cheap; quick; effective sanction on bailiff; may get compensation.

Against: Obscure and little used; no legal aid and may be very high costs if lost.

Complaint to magistrates' court

Any person aggrieved by a levy, or an attempt to levy, for local taxes or child support maintenance can 'appeal' the bailiff's action to the local magistrates' court.

Although the regulations speak of the procedure being used to challenge 'irregularities' alone, it has been decided by the courts that this term actually includes any wrongful act by the bailiff i.e. illegality, irregularity or an excessive levy (see page 138 above).

This statutory remedy does not take away your alternative right to issue a county court claim for damages or to replevy.

The appeal is initiated by making a 'complaint' to the court on a standard form, giving details of the parties, outlining the case and requesting the issue of a claim form directed to the creditor (see example Sample 12, page 155).

At the hearing, if the court is satisfied that the levy was wrongful, it can order the return of the goods distrained. As an alternative to ordering return of goods the court may order an award of compensation for any goods sold by the bailiffs.

It has been decided that the amount of damages that can be awarded can cover all losses caused by the wrongful levy, including damages for annoyance, injury to credit and reputation.

The court can also order the creditor and bailiffs to desist from any levying in an irregular manner and so can benefit everyone living in your area. It must be stressed that the 'appeal' is not a small claim as in the county court.

T **Tips& Hints**

As above, beware paying the other side's legal costs.

If you are not successful, you may well be ordered to pay the other side's legal costs. Once again, careful thought and legal advice may be necessary first.

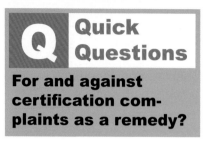

For: Fairly quick and cheap; may recover goods or compensation; bailiff can be told to 'clean up act'.

Against: Magistrates' courts may not be best venue for hearing claim for damages; could be costly if lose.

Interpleader

If goods owned by a third party are seized by a bailiff, the owner has several options.

T Tips& Hints

Use interpleader if the goods seized belonged to you but were seized for the debts of a third party

S/he may issue a claim for wrongful interference; s/he may initiate replevin; in some cases, the remedy of interpleader may also be available. This procedure applies to HCEOs, county court bailiffs and those enforcing road traffic debts.

Note that as mentioned, in chapter 5, this procedure can also be used in the High Court and county court where exempt goods are seized.

Interpleader is a process by which the creditor and a third party make claims against one another (interplead) so that the ownership of the property may be decided by the court. It may also be used by the bailiff to gain protection against other court actions arising out of any substantial grievance caused by his wrongful acts (see 'Damages' later).

Claims to property seized may be made by a wide range of individuals - for example, partners, spouses, relatives, friends, lodgers, trade suppliers, trustees in bankruptcies and hire or HP firms.

The procedure is as follows.

Notice

In all cases, the interpleader claimant should put their claim to the ownership of the goods in writing (see example at Sample13, page 155).

In the High Court the third party must give notice of the claim, including a full description of goods, to the HCEO, who notifies the execution creditor. The judgment creditor must then decide whether to admit the claim or not. If the creditor admits the claim, the HCEO withdraws. If the creditor disputes the claim or fails to reply, the HCEO can apply to the Court for protection against any proceedings relating to the seizure and should withdraw from possession of the goods claimed.

Protection from being sued by the owner will normally be granted but will not be where there is a substantial grievance against the bailiff which seems serious enough to override this immunity. See the case of *Huntress Search v Canapeum Ltd,* mentioned earlier in chapter 5, in which the HCEO was refused this protection because of his conduct.

In the county court the claimant serves notice on a county court district judge if the levying bailiff will not accept his/her claim. The district judge then notifies the creditor. If the claim is admitted the bailiff is withdrawn.

T Tips& Hints

Road traffic cases are more complex

The district judge may then seek protection against claims arising from the disputed seizure. Normally the district judge will be protected but, as with the HCEO, this may be overridden.

Starting off interpleader in High Court and county court cases is quite easy and informal because court proceedings have already been begun. In road traffic cases, interpleader is more complicated because there is not an ongoing county court cases as such. The Traffic Enforcement Centre at Northampton county court has issued an order allowing the traffic authority to enforce the unpaid PCN, but there is no continuing county court claim with a claim number.

This means that to start interpleader in the court you will have to start a completely new county court case. This is done by issuing a Part 8 claim form, asking the court to determine ownership at an interpleader hearing (see figure 14).

Application
In the High Court, if the claim is disputed by the execution creditor the HCEO applies for 'interpleader' and notifies the parties. Within 14 days, the claimant must serve on the other parties an affidavit specifying goods and chattels claimed and the grounds for the claim.

In the county court if no reply is received or the creditor refuses agree to return of the goods then an interpleader claim form is issued on N88 and a hearing is arranged. In road traffic cases a hearing will take place unless the traffic authority responds to the Part 8 claim form by admitting the interpleader claimant's right of ownership of the goods in question.

Security deposit

The High Court may order payment of a deposit or the provision of security, and the county court must require this when accepting any interpleader claim. This requirement does not apply to interpleader against road traffic bailiffs.

The security may be a solicitor's undertaking, a bond from a bank or insurance company or a guarantee from a person with two other sureties.

The purpose of the deposit is to place in the court's control a sum equivalent to the value of the disputed goods and, if the claimant wishes the bailiff to withdraw, a sum representing the costs that the bailiff has incurred up until that date. This fund then becomes the subject matter of the dispute and the goods are released to the claimant and cannot be seized again by that creditor.

In the county court if no deposit is paid the goods must be sold and the proceeds paid into court to await the judge's decision unless the judge decides otherwise in the circumstances. If less than the value is deposited the bailiffs must not withdraw and the court can order the bailiff to retake possession.

Damages

In county court cases the interpleader claimant may claim any damages s/he feels have been incurred, within 8 days of receiving the claim form. In the High Court any such claim for damages must be made in a separate case. If there has been substantial grievance or injury, damages should be awarded.

Factors to be taken into account by the court when considering an award of damages will include:

> where the bailiff has entered the premises of a stranger and seized that person's goods; and,

> where the claim arose from the bailiff's own wrongful actions - for instance, there has been an assault or the goods were seized in the knowledge that they were not yours.

Hearing

A hearing of the contested ownership claim then follows. If the claimant fails to attend or fails to comply with the order made, the Court may bar him/ her from any future claims.

If the execution creditor doesn't appear the HCEO is ordered to withdraw from possession. The HCEO will of course be told to withdraw if the third party's claim is established. If the claimant only establishes ownership of some of the goods, s/he is entitled to be paid from the deposit a sum representing the value of those goods, but the execution creditor will receive the balance. Similar orders may be made in the county court.

Interpleader, especially in the county court, has distinct advantages. It is very simple to initiate and is generally dealt with quite promptly by the court. The procedure is more elaborate in the High Court, although in both cases the bulk of the paperwork and preparation is undertaken by the courts and the HCEO. In road traffic cases, a heavier burden falls on the claimant to the goods who will have to incur the cost and trouble of starting a wholly new claim.

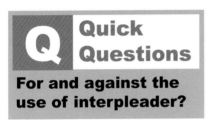

For and against the use of interpleader?

For: Relatively quick way of proving ownership and recovering goods;

Against: Little used and little known; security may be required; may not recover all the goods.

Criminal Remedies

There is no reason why a bailiff acting under a warrant may not commit, or be in danger of committing, a criminal offence.

That said, experience suggests that the police are often reluctant to get involved in anything that may be classed a 'civil dispute' and, other than a warning against a breach of the peace, they are unlikely to take criminal proceedings and will probably advise you to seek a remedy in the civil courts.

If the police are not prepared to act (as is often the case), it will probably be advisable to seek legal advice rather than trying to bring a private prosecution entirely unassisted.

Violent entry

Section 6 Criminal Law Act 1977 makes it an offence for any person to use or threaten violence, without lawful authority, in order to secure entry into any premises. On conviction the person can be fined up to £5000 and/or be sentenced to up to 6 months in prison.

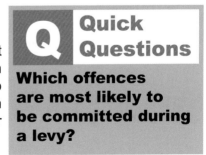

Which offences are most likely to be committed during a levy?

For the entry to be criminal there must be someone on the premises opposed to the entry and the bailiff seeking to enter must know this. The violence must be directed against the premises or person. If such an entry is in progress the police may be called and a constable is empowered to arrest, without warrant, anyone with reasonable cause suspected of committing such an offence. This is thus a very immediate remedy but one seldom likely to be successfully applied.

Criminal damage

An illegal violent entry may also involve criminal damage. This offence arises wherever another's property is intentionally or recklessly destroyed or damaged without lawful excuse, or threats to that effect are made. It would be for the police to pursue a prosecution.

Miscellaneous remedies

Other 'civil' remedies should also be mentioned, although they will very seldom be encountered.

Magistrates' court restitution orders

These can be made against the landlord or bailiff levying distress for rent following a complaint to a magistrates' court made by the aggrieved person. These orders can be made in two situations:

exempt goods have been seized by the landlord
These are the tenant's household goods and tools covered by the statutory exemption (see chapter 5). The court may order either restoration of the goods if not sold or, if they have been disposed of, payment of a sum in compensation by the bailiff; or,

lodger's or stranger's goods
if these are removed by the landlord despite service of the written notice mentioned in chapter 5, application for their recovery can be made to a magistrates' court. After enquiring into the truth of the applicant's declaration and inventory, the court may declare the goods to be exempt from distress and order their return by the bailiff.

In either case if the bailiff does not comply, he faces committal or daily penalties until the goods are returned. The complaint will be on a standard form as in the magistrates appeal described earlier, and will be relatively cheap.

Double damages

In the case of a distress for rent that was illegal because no rent was due, the owner of the goods (whether that is the tenant or third party) has a right by statute to recover damages equal to double the value of goods taken and sold. The offence is not complete unless actual sale occurs, so unfortunately the goods will have to be lost before any right to compensation arises.

If no rent was due, there may be double damages if distress was exercised. Use form N1 to claim

The person would make a county court claim on Part 7 claim form N1.

For and against the use of seeking double damages for rent distress?

For: May offer a quick remedy or compensation.

Against: Mostly obscure and little used.

Conclusions

Readers should remember that:

▶ negotiation is better than confrontation;

▶ informal remedies are better than court;

▶ court can cost you money, even if you win; and,

▶ you will always need a well prepared case and as much proof as you can get.

Bailiffs' Remedies (For & Against)

Remedy	Advantages	Disadvantages
Issue a claim for trespass to land	*Venue* is the county court *Damages* will be awarded: may be exemplary *Injunction* may stop the bailiff returning and removing.	*Court fees* will be payable; *Claim form* must be completed; *Damages* may be low and are only compensation. Lost goods can't be recovered.
Issue a claim for wrongful interference	*Venue* is the county court *Order* damages or goods' return .	*Court fees* will be payable *Claim form* must be drafted
Injunction	*Prevention* of further visits removal, sale etc *Venue* is the county court.	*Cost high*, fees can be waived *Affidavit* must be drafted *Courts* have been reluctant to interfere by this means *Payment of a sum for security* into court may be required *Damages* claim must be prepared at same time.
Replevin	*Recovery* of goods is immediate *Venue* is the county court *Damages* can be recovered.	*Obscure*, two-stage remedy *Deposit is required*, but no fee *Costs* will be high if lose *No standard claim form* is available.
Appeal to the magistrates' court	*Costs* are lower than in the county court and can be waived *Damages* can be awarded *Procedures* can be improved by order of the court *Application* is relatively simple.	*Venue* is the magistrates' court *Costs* can be high if lose.
Pay & claim	*Loss of goods avoided* by up front payment *Venue* is county court *Costs* low as small claim	*Fees* may be payable *Lump sum* needed to pay *Payment under protest* vital.
Interpleader	*Third party* can claim goods *Application* is simple (for court executions) *Venue* is county court	*Only* applies to execution *Payment* into court may be ordered *Road traffic cases* - must issue Part 8 claim.
Complaint to the certificating court	*Venue* is the county court *Application* is simply by letter and there is no fee *Compensation* can be awarded *Bailiff* can lose her/his certificate	*Obscure* remedy, little used *Risk of legal costs*

Bailiffs - The Law and Your Rights

Sample 9
Statement of claim for damages for illegal seizure

IN THE ANYTON COUNTY COURT   Claim no: 11AD12345

Between:

Mr Y XYZ	Claimant

v

Mayor & Burgesses of the Borough of XX	1st defendants

And

ZZ Bailiffs	2nd defendants

Statement of claim

Give statement of events in numbered paragraphs,
1)
2)
describing how distraint was illegal;

3) The claimant has suffered loss, damage and injury as a result of the levy of illegal distraint.

Particulars of damage
1) *Describe losses*
2) *in numbered paragraphs*

4) Further by virtue of s69 County Courts Act 1984 the claimant is entitled to recover and claim interest on the amount found to be due at such rate and for such period as the court shall think fit.

AND the claimant claims:

1) DAMAGES for illegal distress;

2) DAMAGES for assault;

[3) AN INJUNCTION to prevent the second defendant's return or removal of goods]

4) INTEREST thereon, and

5) COURT FEES.

Dated this   day of   201X.

Signed:

Sample 10
Replevin Notice

To the District Judge of Anyton County Court,

TAKE NOTICE that I intend to replevy the goods illegally distrained by xx on xth x.

AND TAKE NOTICE that I intend to commence an action of replevin in the Anyton County Court in which I will be the claimant and YY Borough Council and ZZ Bailiffs will be the defendants.

I apply for security to be fixed for the due prosecution of the proposed action.

Dated the xth day of x 201X.

Signature:

Sample 11
Statement of Claim in Action of Replevin

To the District Judge of Anyton County Court

Give statement of events in numbered paragraphs,
1)
2)
describing how distraint was illegal, that replevin was issued & making claim for damages;

3) The claimant has suffered loss, damage and injury as a result of the levy of illegal distraint.

　　<u>Particulars of damage</u>
　　1) *Describe losses &*
　　2) *Make claim for costs of replevin*

4) The claimant is entitled under section 69 County Courts Act 1984 to claim interest on the amounts found due at such rate and for such period as the court thinks fit.

AND the claimant claims:

1) DAMAGES for illegal distress;
2) COURT FEES;
3) A DECLARATION that the distraint was illegal and cancellation of the replevin bond.

Signed:

Sample 12
Magistrates' Court Appeal

Date: Anyton Magistrates' court

Defendants: London Borough of X
                ZZ Bailiffs

Address: Civic Centre, London

Matter of complaint: An appeal by an aggrieved council tax payer under reg.46 Council Tax (Administration & Enforcement) Regs 1992 [or reg 15 Non Domestic Rating (Collection & Enforcement) (Local Lists) Regs 1989, or reg 31 Child Support (Collection & Enforcement) Regs 1992] following an illegal levy of distress by the defendants.

The complaint of: Ms. Y XYZ

Address: 34, xx Rd, London
who, upon oath, states that the defendants were responsible for the matter of complaint of which particulars are given above.

Taken & sworn before me

.... Justice of the Peace

....Justices Clerk

Sample 13
Interpleader claim

To the District Judge of Anyton County Court

TAKE NOTICE that I, xx, of xx, claim the goods and chattels specified below [or specified in the list attached to this notice] which have been taken by you at xx under a warrant of execution against the goods of yy of yy, as I am given to understand.

The grounds for my claim are as follows:-

Dated the xth day of x 2011.
Signature:

Inventory of goods

Sample 14
Interpleader claim in road traffic cases (Part 8 claim

IN THE ANYTON COUNTY COURT   Claim no: 11AD12345

Between:

Mr Y XYZ   Claimant

v

Mayor & Burgesses of the Borough of XX   1st defendants

And

ZZ Bailiffs   2nd defendants

Statement of claim

Give statement of situation and events in numbered paragraphs,
1)
2)
Setting out how the local authority got a court order from the Traffic Enforcement Centre, how the bailiffs were instructed and how the goods of a third party not liable for the road traffic penalty were seized.

3) The claimant has suffered loss, damage and injury as a result of the levy of illegal distraint.

Particulars of damage
1) *Describe losses*
2) *in numbered paragraphs*

4) Further by virtue of s69 County Courts Act 1984 the claimant is entitled to recover and claim interest on the amount found to be due at such rate and for such period as the court shall think fit.

AND the claimant claims:

1) AN INTERPLEADER ORDER determining the ownership of the goods described;

2) DAMAGES forloss of the use of the goods;

3) *INTEREST thereon; and,*

4) *COURT FEES.*

Dated this   day of   201X.

Signed:

Chapter Nine
Conclusion

The activities of bailiffs are bound to cause controversy, even when they act perfectly correctly.

This inevitable source of contention is compounded by the law, which has been unreformed over centuries and which is complex and confusing, and by the need for the bailiff to try to make money from enforcement work. Where individuals are in genuine financial difficulties, this cannot but exacerbate their situation and aggravate their feelings.

The government has for many years wanted to reform enforcement law. The basis for doing this now exists in an Act of Parliament, the Tribunals, Courts and Enforcement Act 2007. This lays out a new consolidated code of bailiffs' powers, a single, modern fee scale and new provisions on the regulation of bailiffs.

Much of the detail of these new procedures has yet to be agreed, but the Act has the potential to eradicate many sources of dispute. That said, much will depend on how the sector is regulated in future whilst (at the time of writing) the implementation date for the new law has been postponed from April 2012 to an unknown point in the future. No proposals have been made for regulation.

This book can do no better than to conclude with a list of the main points of current bailiff law for which you should watch out and which should be checked against the correct and lawful procedures described in the text.

To conclude, the key points to remember in all dealings with bailiffs are these:

► you should always act early to arrange payment or appeal and avoid enforcement;

► you don't have to open the door (but note the different rules for fines!)

► putting valued goods out of the reach of bailiffs will probably safeguard them;

► if you are concerned over what happens, complain; and,

► if you don't think your complaint is properly resolved, persist and go higher.

Table 8 - Complaints checklist

Action	What to check	Remedy/action if not
Bailiffs instructed	Liability for the debt	Distress is illegal. Notify bailiffs, challenge creditor.
Letters/ initial visits	Content of letters sent/left	Harassment? Warn bailiffs.
	"Constructive levy"	No effect. Notify bailiffs.
Entry	What methods used?	Illegal entry? Issue a claim.
Goods seized	Third party goods?	Issue interpleader, replevin or claim.
	Exempt goods seized?	Illegal seizure. Issue a claim or interpleader.
	Contents of inventory - catch-all phrase used?	Invalid. Warn bailiffs.
	Time elapsed since seizure?	No contact? Abandonment.
Impounding	No or 'verbal' walking possession agreement?	Abandonment? If continued, illegal levy - issue a claim.
	Correct signature on walking possession agreement?	No - abandonment? If continued, illegal levy - issue a claim.
	Proper preliminaries - entry etc.	Invalid levy? If continued, illegal levy - issue a claim.
Removal	Un-listed goods taken?	Illegal removal. Issue a claim.
	Forced entry after invalid seizure?	Illegal removal - issue a claim.
	Third party goods taken?	Interpleader or claim.
Sale	Took too much?	Excessive distress. Issue a claim.
Charges	Sold for undervalue	Irregular distress. Issue a claim.
	Got a copy of the bill?	Ask for one in writing.
Charges (cont)	Got a copy of the fee scale?	Ask for one from the bailiffs or creditors.
	Fees correctly calculated/ applied?	Challenge by detailed assessment or issue a claim.
	Illegal charges made? - fees not on scale? - fees for work not done?	Challenge by detailed assessment or issue a claim.

Appendix One: Quick reference glossary

Bailiff:
   any official employed to seize goods to recover debt.

Close possession:
   impounding where the bailiff remains at the premises guarding the goods.

Distrain:
   a verb meaning the act of seizing goods.

Distraint:
   has the same meaning as distress.

Distress:
   any summary remedy involving seizure of goods outside the civil courts. Distress can mean the process of entry, seizure and impounding (including possible removal) and can mean the goods seized, the actual subject of the distress.

Excessive seizure:
   any levy in which more than is reasonably required is taken.

Execution:
   seizure of goods to enforce a civil court judgment or order (this includes High Court and county court judgments and road traffic penalties). Also, the act of enforcing a warrant to seize goods.

HCEO / High Court enforcement officer:
   the High Court bailiff.

Illegal levy:
   a case where there is no right to levy or where a serious error is committed by the bailiff.

Impounding:
   the act of securing seized goods so that they have legal protection.

Interpleader:
   a remedy for third parties to recover goods wrongly taken in execution.

Irregular seizure:
   a levy where there is a technical error by the bailiff.

Legal custody:
 when goods are impounded in the custody of the law they are protected from rescue and poundbreach and the bailiff will be entitled to force entry in order to remove and sell them.

Levy:
 this word is often interchangeable with the verbs 'distrain', 'seize' and 'execute (a warrant)'. Strictly, it refers to the entire process from entry to sale, but commonly it is applied to the process of seizure and impounding.

PCN:
 a 'penalty charge notice' issued for a parking or traffic contravention by a local authority.

Possession:
 this is now largely interchangeable with 'impounding' and means the process of securing seized goods.

Poundbreach:
 wrongful interference with impounded goods, by the debtor or a third party.

Replevin:
 a remedy to recover goods illegally distrained.

Removal:
 the act of taking seized goods away from the debtor's premises preparatory to sale.

Rescue:
 self-help recovery of seized goods. It may be an offence.

Seizure:
 identifying goods to the value of the debt being collected.

Walking possession:
 impounding where the bailiff leaves the goods at the debtor's premises under an agreement that they have been levied.

Wrongful seizure:
 any levy where a fundamental error is made by the bailiff.

Appendix Two
National Standard for Enforcement Agencies

Key points

General matters

• Agents must not discriminate unfairly on any grounds such as age, disability, race, gender, religion or sexual orientation.

• Agencies must operate & publicise complaints & disciplinary procedures which should be in plain English, have clear contacts & time limits & an independent appeal process where appropriate (e.g. CBA or ACEA schemes).

• Enforcement agents should respect the religion & culture of others at all times. They should be aware of dates for religious festivals & carefully consider the appropriateness of enforcement on any day of religious or cultural observance or during any major religious or cultural festival.

• Agents & creditors should protect the vulnerable & socially excluded & should have procedures to deal with such cases. Those who might be potentially vulnerable include:

  • elderly people;
  • people with disabilities or suffering from serious illness;
  • those recently bereaved;
  • single parent families & pregnant women;
  • unemployed people;
  • those who have obvious difficulty in understanding, speaking or reading English. Agents should if possible be able to rapidly access translation services & provide on request information in large print or in Braille.

• Creditors must be fully aware of their own responsibilities, which should be observed and set out in terms of agreement with their enforcement agent/agency.

Conduct of levies

• Enforcement agents should always produce identification on request, together with a warrant from the creditor.

• Enforcement should not occur on Sundays, Bank Holidays, Good Friday or on Christmas Day, unless a court orders otherwise or legislation permits it.

• Enforcement should only occur between the hours of 6.00am and 9.00pm or at any time outside those hours when the debtor is conducting business.

• Agents should not discuss a case with anyone except the debtor if possible.

• Agents must withdraw if the only person present is, or appears to be, under the age of 18; they can ask when the debtor will be home - if appropriate.

• Enforcement agents must withdraw without making enquiries if the only persons present are children who appear to be under the age of 12.

• Enforcement agents should not remove anything clearly identifiable as an item belonging to, or for the exclusive use of a child.

• Levies should be proportionate to the debt and costs due.

• A receipt should be left for all goods removed and they should be handled with reasonable care to avoid damage whilst in the bailiffs' possession. Bailiffs companies should have insurance in place to cover goods in transit.

• Agents should provide clear & prompt information, should explain the consequences of seizure & the fees charged so far & possible in the future.

• Whenever a fee is incurred, notice of this & previous fees should be given.

• A detailed breakdown of fees should be supplied on receiving a written request.

Appendix 3: Summary of OFT guidance on unfair business practices

This guidance applies to all consumer credit licence holders. To check if a firm is licenced, ring the OFT on: 0207 211 8608.

Communication
It is unfair to communicate, in whatever form, with consumers in an unclear, inaccurate or misleading manner. Examples include:

• use of official looking documents intended or likely to mislead debtors as to their status e.g. documents made to resemble court claims;

• leaving out or presenting information in such a way that it creates a false or misleading impression or exploits debtors' lack of knowledge;

• those contacting debtors not making clear who they are, who they work for, what their role is, what the purpose of the contact is; and,

• contacting debtors at unreasonable times.

False representation of authority and/or legal position
Those contacting debtors must not deceitfully misrepresent their authority and/or the correct legal position. Examples include:

• implying or claiming authority, e.g. claiming to work on instructions from the courts;

• implying or stating that action can be taken when it legally cannot; and,

• implying or stating that failure to pay a debt is a criminal offence or that criminal proceedings will be brought.

Physical/psychological harassment
Putting pressure on debtors is considered to be oppressive. Examples include:

• contacting debtors at unreasonable times and at unreasonable intervals;

• making threatening statements or gestures or taking actions which suggest harm to debtors;

• ignoring and/ or disregarding claims that debts have been settled, or are disputed, and continuing to make demands for payment;

• acting in a way likely to be publicly embarrassing to the debtor, either deliberately or through lack of care, e.g. by not posting correspondence in a sealed envelope running the risk that it could be read by third parties.

Charging for debt collection
Charges should not be levied unfairly. Examples include:

- claiming collection costs in the absence of express legal provision;

- applying unreasonable charges, e.g. charges not based on actual and necessary costs; and,

- applying charges which are disproportionate to the main debt.

Debt collection visits
Those visiting debtors must not act in an unclear or threatening manner e.g.:

- visiting a debtor when it is known they are vulnerable;

- continuing with a visit when it becomes apparent that the debtor is distressed or otherwise vulnerable, e.g. it becomes apparent that the debtor has mental health problems;

- not leaving a property when asked to do so.

Appendix 4 - Further reading & websites

Books

John Kruse, *Law of seizure of goods*, 2nd edition, Hammicks, 2009; *Powers of distress - a guide to the remedies unreformed by the Tribunals, Courts & Enforcement Act 2007*, Wildy, Simmonds & Hill, 2009; *Bailiffs' law (a history of the development of the law), two volumes*, Wildy, Simmonds & Hill, 2009;

Various authors, *Debt advice handbook*, Child Poverty Action Group, 2010.

Websites

High Court Enforcement Officers Association- www.hceoa.org.uk

For all forms: Her Majesty's Court Service- www.hmcourts-service.gov.uk

BAILII - www.bailii.org

Certified bailiffs information – www.hmcourts-service.gov.uk/CertificatedBailiffs/

Complaints about certified bailiffs – www.hmcourts-service.gov.uk/courtfinder/forms/form4_0606.pdf

Government legislation - www.legislation.gov.uk

Civil Procedure Rules - www.justice.gov.uk/civil/procrules_fin/

Criminal Procedure Rules - www.justice.gov.uk/criminall/procrules_fin/index.htm

Local Government Ombudsman - www.lgo.org.uk

Parliamentary Ombudsman - www.ombudsman.org.uk

Revenues Adjudicator- www.adjudicatorsoffice.org.uk

Forums: see inside back page for details of CAG forum on bailiffs

Index